PLAY
WINNING
BRIDGE

PLAY WINNING BRIDGE

with any partner

EVEN A STRANGER

By

Chas H Goren

CORNERSTONE LIBRARY   NEW YORK

CORNERSTONE LIBRARY PUBLICATIONS
Are Distributed By
Simon & Schuster Inc.
630 Fifth Avenue
New York, New York 10020

Manufactured in the United States of America
under the supervision of
Rolls Offset Printing Co., Inc., N. Y.

CONTENTS

Foreword

THE SEARCH for an international language has been going on for many years. One of the early experimenters was a Dr. Zamenhoff, who in 1887 offered up his own codification which was known as Esperanto. The title was based on a Spanish word, meaning hope. But despite the sincere efforts of the founder and those who followed the hope was never realized. There have no doubt been earlier efforts dating as far back as the tower of Babel, but all met with similar lack of success.

Gradually there appears to me to be looming a slight ray of hope. My view is based on personal experiences in far corners of this planet. In my salad days, I made some pretense at Latin and Greek, aspiring even to teach these languages. Later I studied French and even put it mildly to use during my college days at McGill University in Montreal. But presently this knowledge has left me. I have retained only enough Greek to permit a relaxed passage inside fraternity row at most colleges; I can still recall a few scattered passages from the Aeneid, and if the waiter has a smattering of clairvoyance I can get by with ordering a meal in France. But that is the limit of my linguistic talents.

Yet I have fared rather well in many lands for a number of years. What is the secret? Contract Bridge!

The carping critic will, of course, dilute my story by pointing out that in all international tournaments English is the official language. But I have participated in local tournaments (these have been staged in Norway, Sweden, Switzerland, Spain, France and Italy) where only the native language is spoken, with a minimum number of disasters due to lapsi lingual.

Throughout these pages you will note my drive for simplicity. In the decades that preceded me, the leading authorities of the day were subjected to criticism for frequent changes allegedly calculated to drum up sales.

I, however, have preferred to stand pat. One of my most successful books, Point Count Bidding, made its official appearance in 1949, though I had been experimenting with it for several years. Now, over a dozen years later, I may suggest that the original edition would serve reasonably well as a guide for today.

I believe in giving aid and comfort to my friends and never for an instant do I take my eyes off the ultimate goal of Contract Bridge, which as I see it is the reaping of pleasure.

At the conclusion of my weekly television program, Championship Bridge with Charles Goren over the ABC network, I devote about a minute for a tip on bridge. I should like to adopt that practice right here, and in conclusion give you perhaps the most important tip within my reach, and that is: "have fun."

PLAY
WINNING
BRIDGE

1. *Establishing Cozy Relationships*

LORD CHESTERFIELD once advised very sharply against associating in business enterprises with anyone who appears to be chronically unlucky. He did not elaborate on his thesis but a between-the-lines reading of his words makes it appear that he did not really believe in luck. What he intended to transmit to his audience was the thought that those who are consistently unlucky would do well to have a thorough check-up on the techniques they are employing. It is perhaps time for a visit to the local pro to determine what has happened to the swing.

In open games where you select your partner each rubber by cutting cards, the luck of the cut is perhaps as important as the luck of the cards which are dealt to you. This observation does not apply with equal force in a pivot game where one plays every fourth rubber with the same partner. In that type of game one must adjust to variations of quality.

Not infrequently the weak sister at the table will be the most temperamental, and when you draw him as your partner you will give yourself a decided advantage if you establish cordial relations with him at the start. Be quick with your compliments and hold back your rebukes. When he has just managed to be set on a "laydown" hand it will be to your advantage not to have noticed the play.

If you are confronted head on with the question "Could I have made it, partner?" you may find yourself in a trap. The white lie is not recommended at this juncture, for some helpful kibitzer or even one of your opponents will point out very simply how the hand could have been made, and the damage to your face will be irreparable. You may say, I think, "It could be made if you knew where all the cards were." I deliberately avoid the use of the expression "double dummy" because of the connotation carried by this term.

One of the early champions of the game, and a highly favored partner of mine in the decade of the thirties, was Charles Lochridge, whose charming manner at times concealed a vitriolic nature. He had been obliged to sit quietly by as his partner committed mayhem on some simple hand and went down one on a contract that was known to the profession as a "spread." "Well, what is your comment, partner?" he was asked. "Only this," retorted Lochridge. "At double dummy you could have gone down two."

It is important never to lose sight of the fundamental principle that Contract Bridge is a game of communication, and you must not submit messages which the inexperienced player will have difficulty decoding. Don't tell the neophyte what you want him to do. It will be much easier and surely more profitable for you to adjust to his methods however bizarre they seem to be. This may appear to be a statement against self interest, for on the surface it might be more desirable to promote my own system. Yet the cozy atmosphere is fostered by informing your partner that he is not only the captain of his soul but the master of his fate. When I cut a partner who promises to play "straight Goren" I always act deeply grateful, though I may take it with a grain of salt. I nevertheless adhere religiously to all the tenets which I have inscribed for what I hoped would be posterity.

A few random tips:

To Husbands playing with their wives: Be slow to take control. Remember, it is barely possibly that the Madam plays as well as you do. In fact, from what I have read, the odds incline that way.

To the Wife: Ladies, you don't have to tell me. I've already gone on record countless times, to the effect that you play better than your husband. You and I know it, but try not to let him find out. It may lead to his giving up the game, and that is decidedly against my interests.

Let me refer you to the philosophy of Maggie Wylie, J. M. Barrie's delightful character in *What Every Woman Knows*. "Every man who is high up loves to think that he has done it all himself and the wife smiles and lets it go at that. It's our only joke. Every woman knows that."

Don't be a Talent Scout

Unless you have been engaged in a professional capacity, teaching is not a rewarding profession—in bridge particularly—and is probably one of the most effective means of alienating your friends.

When your friend and neighbor, Mrs. Jones, has brought her husband to the party for the purpose of completing a table, you will no doubt get him as your partner. Let me beseech you to avoid concerning yourself with his education as a bridge player. And if he is so far advanced as to discuss conventions make it easy for him. Do it his way.

The Stayman convention may come up for discussion and there it is possible that you will be stepping on thin ice. Don't ever refuse to play the gadget which has been suggested by partner. He would straightway peg you as stuffy if you did. Simply plead ignorance and courteously ask him to explain it to you. In the time consumed by this pedagogic process, his ardor may be dampened, and you will soon find that he has decided to abandon his newly acquired toys in favor of the simple life.

If it becomes apparent that the language of uptown bridge is not to become part of his repertoire, accept it philosophically and adopt some of the following tips.

Let us assume you have opened with one no trump (a not uncommon occurrence when you are playing with a partner of limited experience), and Mr. Jones responds two spades. You and I know that in the language employed by us in our everyday affairs, this bid strongly urges the opening no trumper to pass. But playing with Mr. Jones one would be risking his financial security by passing. Jones might have a hand which will produce a slam, and one of his neighbors recently told him he must take things easy.

Here is an oft played record:

Opener	Responder
1 NT	2 ♠
2 NT	

This is a great mistake and is apt to get you nowhere. If he now bids three spades you won't be quite sure that he isn't trying to impress you with the power of his suit. If you quit he'll say, "I didn't think you would pass, partner, as long as I kept on bidding." On the other hand, if you carry on to game, a resounding double by the adversary will make it painfully clear that the poor fellow was just looking for a place to park. What should you do in this situation? I think

I have a sure cure for it. When the uncertain partner takes out your bid of one no trump to two spades, raise him to three without bothering to look at your hand again.

If he had a hand replete with high cards he'll surely return to three no trump, for he never at any time had the desire to play in spades, he was just showing you his suit. If he had a weak hand containing a spade suit he'll probably quit—no disaster. If he had a hand with a good spade suit he'll go on to four.

You are in effect putting him through the lie detector test, and you'll be surprised how often the truth will out.

This is equally true if he bids two hearts or two diamonds over your opening one no trump. Suppose, though, he bids two clubs. Perhaps you *should* ask him whether or not he plays this rather new convention —that is, unless he asks you first.

The Two Club Convention

The two club bid is used in response to an opening bid of one no trump and requests the opening bidder to show a four card major suit if he has one. If not, he is expected to bid two diamonds which is artificial and merely denies the majors.

The two club bidder should have a minimum of eight high card points as well as at least four cards in one of the majors.

After opener's rebid, the responder should assume control. With ten points or more he should make a jump bid to assure reaching a game contract. With eight or nine points he either raises opener's major suit or else returns to two no trump.

Proper use of this device produced a crucial swing for one team on a hand taken from a recent match.

East-West vulnerable. South deals.

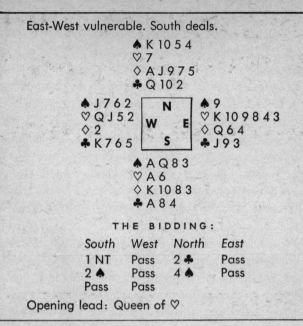

♠ K 10 5 4
♡ 7
◇ A J 9 7 5
♣ Q 10 2

♠ J 7 6 2   ♠ 9
♡ Q J 5 2   ♡ K 10 9 8 4 3
◇ 2   ◇ Q 6 4
♣ K 7 6 5   ♣ J 9 3

♠ A Q 8 3
♡ A 6
◇ K 10 8 3
♣ A 8 4

THE BIDDING:

South	West	North	East
1 NT	Pass	2 ♣	Pass
2 ♠	Pass	4 ♠	Pass
Pass	Pass		

Opening lead: Queen of ♡

In the sequence shown above, North's two club bid is artificial and requests his partner to show a biddable four card major suit. South rebid two spades which North cheerfully raised to game.

South won the queen of hearts lead in his hand and laid down the ace-queen of trumps. When East showed out, declarer abandoned the suit temporarily, shifting to king and a small diamond. West discarded on the second lead and the ace won in the dummy. A diamond was returned and East was in with the queen. A heart was led to shorten dummy's trumps. Declarer countered by playing another diamond. West trumped in but could not prevent declarer from taking ten tricks now.

At the other table, North raised South's opening no trump bid directly to three. Even though they were not using the two club convention, they might have reached the four spade contract, had North chosen a three diamond response for which he had the required ten points. South could now bid three spades just as a check back on the way to no trump and North, of course, would choose the suit contract. Despite his five-card diamond holding, so suitable for a no trump contract, the holding of four spades opposite partner's announced four spades, and the singleton heart, make four spades an absolute preference.

West opened the deuce of hearts against three no trump. Since this apparently marked him with four of the suit and East with six, declarer felt that if anyone were short in diamonds, it would be East. So he cashed the king of diamonds first and when West showed out on the next lead, the contract was down one.

North contended that his partner should have played spades first, and there is no doubt that this would have been sound policy. It is always wise to give the defense a chance to make a mistake. In this case if East discards properly, South will still have the diamond guess. At four spades he could afford to lose a diamond trick and still make the hand.

The next anecdote is something in the nature of a confession.

I sat in the traditional South position facing perhaps the most devoted friend I have ever had. An enormously successful tycoon, he was unfortunately unable to cope with the problems one encounters at the bridge table. Success in his chosen field had made him immune to technical advice, and his vast resources induced a looseness in bidding which was trying to his partners, among whom I found myself with great frequency.

I soon learned that my emphatic instructions were destined to fall upon deaf ears.

Neither vulnerable.

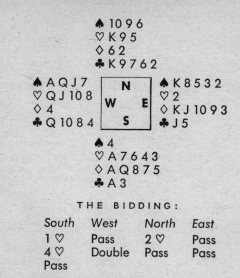

♠ 10 9 6
♡ K 9 5
◇ 6 2
♣ K 9 7 6 2

♠ A Q J 7
♡ Q J 10 8
◇ 4
♣ Q 10 8 4

♠ K 8 5 3 2
♡ 2
◇ K J 10 9 3
♣ J 5

♠ 4
♡ A 7 6 4 3
◇ A Q 8 7 5
♣ A 3

THE BIDDING:

South	West	North	East
1 ♡	Pass	2 ♡	Pass
4 ♡	Double	Pass	Pass
Pass			

Opening lead: Queen of ♡

The hand shown is the first of a rubber which stands out in my memory. I opened with a heart and after a single raise leaped to game. I am, of course, not arguing for the soundness of my bid; a rebid by me at the three level would have done justice to the holding. West doubled and the contract was set two tricks for a sting of 300 points. My tycoon friend did not permit this indiscretion to go unnoticed, and in retort I pointed out that this was my style, and that I couldn't help it if I had inherited over-bidding tendencies from a free and easy father. This alerted my companion to the necessity for holding the middle of the road, and for the remainder of the session he was well in hand. The 300 points proved to be a sound investment.

The moral of the story is this: Don't compensate for an overbidding partner by underbidding yourself. He will sense what you are doing and as a consequence will persist more than ever in his overbidding practices. Equally, don't compensate for an underbidding partner by overbidding yourself.

Sacrificing

The proper use of sacrificing tactics may make the difference between a winner and a loser in a session of play. If by incurring a loss of one or two hundred points you can prevent the opposition from running off with the rubber, obviously that money is well spent. But to prolong the rubber by taking a series of sets ranging from 500 to 700 points or more is palpably unprofitable. It is the stubborn persistence of players who refuse to accept fate that leads to these three- and four-thousand-point rubbers.

On the whole, it is my impression that sacrifice bidding is overdone. In order for it to pay, one must be certain that the opposition can fulfill their contract. There are few experiences more frustrating than incurring a large penalty to save the game only to learn that the opponents could not have made the game for which they had contracted. If there is even a moderate chance to defeat the opponents it is better not to sacrifice. It is sound practice to avoid taking a deliberate loss while there still remains a chance to show a profit.

How much should one be willing to spend in an effort to prevent the opponents from scoring game or rubber? That varies with conditions. In duplicate bridge, where the values of games are arbitrarily assigned, the defenders know exactly how much they can afford to lose depending on conditions of vulnerability. But in rubber bridge there is no way to determine the exact value of the game. Only estimates are available, and these may be reached by judging the worth of the average rubber. Some authorities believe that the average rubber amounts to about 1,000 points. On that basis it would appear that to save the first game a cost of 300 points appears reasonable, while a set of 500 points is a little too high. When both sides are vulnerable and the rubber is immediately at stake, a penalty of 500 points does not appear to be exorbitant.

There is a common misconception to the effect that when the opponents are vulnerable and you are not, great liberties may be taken with sacrifice bids. Nothing could be further from the truth. That is just the time not to sacrifice. When the opposition has a game in, the odds are three to one that they will win the rubber. This is true, because you must win two games in a row. Since you have only one chance in four to pull the rubber out of the fire, it is silly for you to invest money in such a losing proposition. It would pay you to lose a small rubber. Get a fresh start, and if you win the next two games you will have a 700 rubber of your own.

In the chapters that follow I've tried to illuminate more fully those areas which cause the greatest partnership misunderstanding. The French have an expression, *Dialogue des sourds*, conversation of the deaf ones, which might very well, unfortunately, fit a great many bridge partnerships.

The clan of players who long ago took pride in never having read a book, stoutly maintained that they "played by ear." With this latter practice I never took issue, for listening to the bidding is a very vital phase of bridge activity. The eyes and the ears combine to make a formidable team.

Howard Dietz, one of the really experienced bridge players of the entertainment world, tells of an experience he had while partnered with the late Sigmund Romberg, who was a contract enthusiast of great proportions, known for his melodic contributions in the field of American musical plays. Romberg had a way of audibly counting trumps when he was declarer. On the occasion in question Romberg found himself in a four spade contract, and his partner, Dietz, in the dummy seat observed that Sigmund had miscounted trumps and was on the verge of permitting a solitary spade to remain outstanding. The safety of the contract was thus threatened, and Dietz resorted to desperate measures. Leaning back in his chair he started to whistle "One Alone," the hit number from the *Desert Song*.

Unmindful of the suggestion from his anxious partner, Romberg continued to play along until at long last the outstanding trump was put to good use by the defender, and the four spade contract went on the rocks.

With tears in his voice Dietz pleaded, "Sigmund, I tried to be helpful as I whistled one of your great tunes, 'One Alone.' Couldn't you get the idea?" Romberg, a musician to the end, merely retorted, "Who knows from lyrics?"

2. *Forcing Bids*

ALTHOUGH THE SUBJECT of forcing bids has been dealt with at considerable length in the texts, failure to apply properly the principles and rules contained therein has been the source of much confusion and consequently partnership disasters at the bridge table.

The distinction between which bids are forcing and which are highly invitational, not to mention those that are only mildly encouraging, is by no means perfectly clear even to the more experienced players. It might therefore prove to be a very refreshing pause if we take time out for a moment to review the subject.

There are two general classifications of forcing bids:

1] Those which are forcing to game
2] Those which are forcing for one round.

Game Forcing Bids

We all know, of course, that an opening demand bid (two of a suit) must be kept open until a game contract has been reached (or until the opponents have been doubled in a bid of their own).

Any cue bid of an opponent's suit is a game force.

Any jump shift is forcing to game if partner has bid voluntarily.

A jump bid by the responder at any time in the auction is forcing to game, *provided* that he has not previously passed.

After the opening bidder has made a strength-showing rebid, such as a jump in no trump or a jump in his own suit, if the responder elects to bid again, the partnership is committed to game. When both players have bid strongly, the bids are presumed to be forcing to game.

One Round Forces

A] Every time the responding hand bids a new suit (provided he has not previously passed) the opener must bid once more.

This rule, however, has some exceptions. A response in a new suit is not forcing when made directly over an intervening takeout double. Holding ten points or more, the partner of the opening bidder would redouble. Similarly, if the intervening bid was a one no trump overcall, he would double for penalties with a fair hand. If he bids two of a suit, it shows distributional rather than high card values and the opening bidder is not obligated to go on.

A response of two diamonds, two hearts, or two spades to an opening bid of one no trump shows less than eight points and requests the no trump bidder to retire from the auction. A response of two clubs is forcing for one round and asks the no trump bidder to show a major suit.

Another instance in which the bid of a new suit by the responder is *not* forcing occurs when the opener rebids one no trump.

North	South
1 ♢	1 ♡
1 NT	2 ♣ (not forcing)

In order to force in this sequence, South is obliged to bid three clubs over one no trump.

B] When an opening bid in a major suit has been raised, the bid of a new suit by the opener is forcing for one round.

North	South
1 ♡	2 ♡
3 ♢	?

South must bid once more. Hearts are the agreed trumps and the responder is obliged to return to that suit even if he has no further ambitions.

Summing Up:

Study carefully the forcing situations. Know when you must bid and when you may pass. When you have a hand that appears to be practically worthless and your partner makes a strong bid, do the following things:

1] Determine in your own mind if his bid is forcing

2] If it is, *bid.*

Don't become hysterical and forget the language. Don't be like the conductor in Ernest Newman's delightful anecdote whose use of English was barely adequate when conducting the Covent Garden orchestra. He became exasperated with the orchestra's habit of chattering during a rehearsal, and finally burst out: "Don't spoke! I can stand it then and now but always, my God, never!"

3. *Doubles*

PROBABLY THERE IS NO MORE revealing or profitable message in bridge than "Double"—let's examine some of the language.

"Partner, I am sure that you understand my double is made as a request for you to bid. Announce your best suit and do not panic merely because you have a bad hand. I have made allowance for that development in planning my own bidding, and if I have placed you in an uncomfortable position it will hurt for only just a moment. If I don't have ample support for the suit you pick, I shall produce a reasonably good one of my own with which to rescue you."

Never be heard to say, "Partner, I know your double was for a takeout but I had nothing to bid." A pass at a time like this will brand you as totally unsuited for this game of contract bridge. Make the most appropriate bid in the circumstances and worry about the consequences later.

Now a word to refresh your memory on the nature of the takeout double.

Takeout Doubles

The takeout double says: "Partner, please tell me something about your hand regardless of its weakness. I have a good hand and am prepared to cope with any response."

When is it made?
A double is for a takeout when

1] The double is of one, two or three of a suit.*
2] The double was made at the doubler's first opportunity.
3] Partner has not bid, doubled the opponents, or made a penalty pass.

What are the requirements?

At least 13 points including distribution, in other words, a hand of opening bid strength. Adequate support for any suit partner might bid, or a good suit of your own

♠ A x x x ♡ A Q x x ◇ x ♣ Q 10 9 x

The opening bid on your right is one diamond. This is a splendid type of double. You are prepared for anything.

♠ A Q 10 x ♡ A K Q x x ◇ x x x ♣ x

With this hand you should double even though you have no support for clubs. If partner responds in that suit you can conveniently bid two hearts. The double may serve to uncover a spade fit.

And don't forget, a player who has made a takeout double can repeat his message if his partner fails to speak the first time.

♠ A K x x ♡ K Q J x ◇ x ♣ A 10 9 x

East	South	West	North
1 ◇	Double	2 ◇	Pass
Pass	?		

South should double again to force a bid from partner. Offensive prospects need not be abandoned even though North was unable to bid the first time.

* In our own methods the double of a three bid is intended primarily for takeout, but partner is permitted some leeway in deciding whether to pass and play for a penalty.

Warning:

Always expect partner to respond in your shortest suit. If his bid will prove embarrassing, you should avoid making a takeout double even if you have a good hand.

♠ A K 10 x   ♡ x   ◇ K x x x   ♣ A J x x

If the opening bid on your right was one spade, a pass is recommended, for if you double, partner is apt to respond with two hearts over which you have no convenient escape. Bide your time.

Now let's switch to the partner of the takeout doubler. He is thinking: My hand didn't look like much before, but things are picking up.

When partner doubles, how do you assess your hand?

  6 points, you have a fair hand,
  9 points, you have a good hand,
 11 points, you have a probable game.

If you have more than 11 points, game becomes a moral certainty, provided you reach the proper contract.

You must bid, no matter how bad your hand. The only excuse for passing the double of a one bid, is the belief that you can defeat the opponents. In order to cherish such a belief, you need four tricks, three of which must be in the trump suit.

Responding with a bad hand is merely a technical procedure—an answer to partner's questionnaire. He has promised to take care of any situation that develops, and your job is to inform him of your best suit even if it is not normally biddable.

Here are a few characteristic examples of responding to doubles.

Partner doubles one heart. What is your response with:

A] ♠ x x x ♡ x x x ◇ x x x ♣ x x x x
B] ♠ K J x ♡ 10 x x x x ◇ x x ♣ x x x
C] ♠ Q x x x ♡ x ◇ Q x x x x ♣ J 10 x
D] ♠ K x x ♡ J 10 x x ◇ A x ♣ x x x x

A] Bid two clubs, your longest suit. Remember, you
are obliged to bid no matter how weak your
hand is;

B] Bid one spade. It's not much but it's the best
you can do. You can't pass, because you lack
the required defensive strength;

C] Bid one spade. When the response can be made
at the level of one, a four card major is preferred to a five card minor. The double of one
major suit usually shows support for the other
major;

D] Bid one no trump. In response to a takeout double this bid designates a fairly good hand—
about 8 points.

When to Bid No Trump

Where doubler's partner has a choice between no
trump and a minor suit, he should bid no trump.
Where the choice is between no trump and a major suit
he should bid the major suit.

Partner doubles 1 heart.

♠ 10 x x x ♡ K Q x ◇ K x ♣ 10 9 x x

Bid one spade rather than one no trump.

♠ x x ♡ Q J 9 x ◇ A J 10 x ♣ x x x

Bid one no trump.

How do you show that you're interested?

When you hold 11 points or more and your partner has doubled, you may manifest your interest by
jumping the bid.

Partner doubles one diamond.

♠ x x x   ♡ A x   ◊ A J x x   ♣ K 10 x x

Bid two no trump. You have 12 high card points.

♠ K Q x x x   ♡ x x   ◊ A 10 x x   ♣ x x

Bid two spades. You have 11 points, 9 in high cards
and one for each doubleton.

♠ K 10 x x   ♡ A x x   ◊ Q 10 x   ♣ K x x

Bid two spades, despite the weak suit. You have 12
points and partner should be informed of your strength
directly.

How do you show that you're intensely interested?

Occasionally the doubler's partner wishes to inform the doubler that game is assured even though the
best contract has not yet been determined. In such cases
he may cue bid the opponent's suit whether he has
first-round control or not, in order to get the doubler
to select a suit.

West	North	East	South
1 ♣	Double	Pass	?

♠ A 10 x x   ♡ K J x x   ◊ Q J 10 x   ♣ x

South should respond with a cue bid of two clubs,
since he is ready to carry on to game in any suit partner
bids. The cue bid in clubs may be regarded as a white
lie.

So remember:

When your partner makes a takeout double of one of
a suit, it is depriving him of his franchise for you to
pass and let the opponent play the one contract doubled
just because you happen to be frightened.

But a distinction is to be noted between doubles of
one of a suit and doubles of one no trump. Normally,

severe damage will not be inflicted upon the suit bidder at this low level. But at no trump, where the bidder is subject to attack from all four directions, heavy penalties can be inflicted even at the one level, which leads us to this general conclusion:

Doubles of one no trump should be left in unless the hand is completely unsuitable to defensive play, in which case doubler's partner should bid his long suit.

The arithmetic of the situation is relatively simple. An immediate double of one no trump indicates about 16 points. If doubler's partner has 6, almost the entire pack has been accounted for and dummy will be virtually trickless. Declarer will, therefore, find playing the hand a highly doubtful pleasure.

North-South vulnerable. South deals.

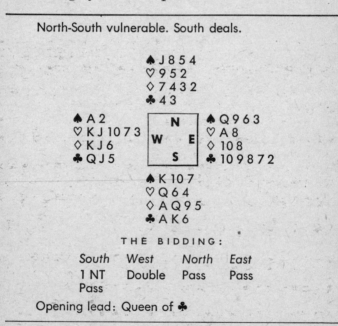

♠ J 8 5 4
♡ 9 5 2
◇ 7 4 3 2
♣ 4 3

♠ A 2
♡ K J 10 7 3
◇ K J 6
♣ Q J 5

♠ Q 9 6 3
♡ A 8
◇ 10 8
♣ 10 9 8 7 2

♠ K 10 7
♡ Q 6 4
◇ A Q 9 5
♣ A K 6

THE BIDDING:

South	West	North	East
1 NT	Double	Pass	Pass
Pass			

Opening lead: Queen of ♣

Here we record one of the bloodiest incidents that has ever come to our attention at this level. South's no trump opening, based on a point count of 18, was surely above reproach, as was West's double. East, having the prescribed 6 points, decided to leave the double in and West made the inspired lead of the queen of clubs. He eschewed the heart suit for fear of leading into a major tenace in declarer's hand.

Declarer won with the king and started on his long suit by playing the ace and another diamond. West won and continued with the club jack. Declarer held off until the third round and cleared the diamonds. But he was unable to make any more tricks. The clubs and hearts and the ace of spades gave the balance to the defense for a net loss of 1,100 points.

South, to be sure, was an innocent victim, but this does not deprive East and West of the credit for gathering rosebuds, while the gathering was good.

The takeout doubler should always exercise caution in rebidding. He has forced partner to speak and partner's bid may have been uttered with considerable reluctance. The doubler therefore should not take any subsequent offensive action that is not justified on the basis of his own hand.

In order to raise partner to

The 2 level—doubler needs 16 points
The 3 level—doubler needs 19 points
The 4 level—doubler needs 22 points.
The bidding has gone:

East	South	West	North
1 ♡	Double	Pass	1 ♠
Pass	?		

As South you hold:

A] ♠ A x x ♡ x x ◇ A K x x ♣ Q J x x
B] ♠ A Q x x ♡ x x ◇ K Q x ♣ A J x x
C] ♠ A K Q x ♡ x ◇ Q J x x ♣ A J x x

A] Pass. There are no bright prospects on this hand. You have a minimum double and partner did not jump the bid, so he has less than 11 points;

B] Bid two spades. Even though you have 17 points, partner may have little or nothing. If he has 9 points he will be heard from again;

C] A raise to three spades is sufficient. You have 20 points in support and a jump raise will appraise partner of this fact.

A good rule of thumb to remember is that in the later rounds of bidding the doubler should make it a practice to underbid, while the doubler's partner should tend to overbid. Too frequently in real life, it is just the other way around.

Let's switch sides now and see what the opening bidder's partner should do over an intervening takeout double.

The proper procedure when partner's opening bid has been doubled by second hand is not always clearly indicated. The advice generally handed out for public consumption is, by and large, in a muddled state.

One particular superstition that seems to have gained quite a foothold is one to the effect that "a bid over a double shows weakness." To this view, of course, we do not subscribe. If you bid over a double, it ought to be for some purpose other than to announce your complete despair. Even with a weak hand you may serve the best interests of your partnership by making a barricade bid to annoy the enemy, but to bid some suit just because you have a bust and to remain quiet because you have a fair to middling hand does not recommend itself to our sense of business.

Simply stated, here is the general procedure when partner's opening bid has been doubled:

1] With a good hand you redouble.

2] With an in-between hand you should bid at once, else you might find it inconvenient to enter the auction on the next round if the action has been fomented.

3] With a poor hand, the proper procedure is to pass unless you are able to give partner a distributional raise.

If a player chooses to bid his own suit over the double, he confesses that his hand does not justify a redouble; that is, it is not above average strength (10 points). But that is by no means bidding to show weakness.

Neither vulnerable. South deals.

```
                 ♠ K J 8 7 2
                 ♡ Q 4 3
                 ◇ 3
                 ♣ J 9 8 2
   ♠ A Q 6 3      ┌─────┐      ♠ 10 5 4
   ♡ K 10 8       │  N  │      ♡ J 9 6 2
   ◇ A Q J 10    W│     │E     ◇ K 8 4 2
   ♣ Q 7          │  S  │      ♣ 6 4
                 └─────┘
                 ♠ 9
                 ♡ A 7 5
                 ◇ 9 7 6 5
                 ♣ A K 10 5 3
```

THE BIDDING:

South	West	North	East
1 ♣	Double	1 ♠	Pass
2 ♣	2 ◇	3 ♣	Pass
Pass	Pass		

In this hand, North's action was quite proper. When partner's club bid was doubled, he reasoned that he had neither a good hand nor a bad one, but surely enough values to justify making his presence known. The important consideration, however, was that if he waited the bidding might reach too high a level for him to enter the auction with safety. After partner had rebid clubs he felt justified in giving a competitive raise to three clubs. There was no danger that South would expect to find a very strong dummy, for it must be borne in mind that North failed to redouble on the first round so that he is definitely on record as having denied possession of a strong hand.

When partner utters a bid that is somewhat out of the ordinary routine, it is well to pause for a moment and ask yourself, "I wonder what he means?" Such a pause might have refreshed the South player of the next hand and saved him several hundred points.

Both vulnerable. South deals.

```
              ♠ Q J 9 4 3
              ♡ 7
              ◇ 6 5 2
              ♣ Q 7 5 3
  ♠ 8                        ♠ 6 5 2
  ♡ A K Q 8      N           ♡ J 9 4 3 2
  ◇ Q J 9 7 4  W   E         ◇ 10 8
  ♣ A J 6        S           ♣ K 10 8
              ♠ A K 10 7
              ♡ 10 6 5
              ◇ A K 3
              ♣ 9 4 2
```

THE BIDDING:

South	West	North	East
1 ♠	Double	3 ♠	Pass
4 ♠	Double	Pass	Pass
Pass			

West's double of the opening bid would be approved by even the most conservative trust company. It was rather easy for North to sense that the opposition probably held a game hand against him and in an effort to block out the expected heart response, he properly leaped to three spades. He was tempted to go the whole way with a bid of four, but considerations of vulnerability deterred him. The loss might be too heavy. East, of course, had not sufficient values for a free bid at that level and was obliged to pass. Had South passed, West would really have been "fixed." It is somewhat doubtful that he would have had the temerity to complete at this level with a passing partner, and South might have bought the hand for the bargain price of 100 points.

South looked at his hand and saw four quick tricks. Pride got the better of him and he went to game for a loss of 500 points. His judgment was not of the best. He should have stopped to ask himself whether his partner had a good hand and the answer would have been, "No." If North had a good hand there was a very simple bid available to him. The redouble. His failure to employ this weapon indicates plainly that he is nervous about it all and is trying to impede the opposition.

A jump bid in this position is not indicative of strength. It is elementary tactics that when your partner's opening bid is doubled by the next player and you have a good hand, you redouble and do the rest of your bidding on subsequent rounds.

South might have adopted a sounder attitude had he valued his hand on a point count basis. He would have observed that his holding was worth only 14 points, barely a mandatory bid. He would perhaps have realized the futility of looking to the North hand to produce 12.

Penalty Doubles

Here's a different message: "We've got 'em, partner. They've stuck their necks way out. Let's collect some points above the line."

When is this interesting proposition suggested?
A double is for penalties (as distinguished from a double for a takeout):

1] Whenever the double is of a four level contract, or higher
2] Whenever the double is of a no trump bid
3] Whenever the doubler has had the previous opportunity to double that suit but failed to do so
4] Whenever the doubler's partner has previously made a bid, doubled or passed for penalties.

When to Double for Penalties

A] If your partner opens the bidding and your right-hand opponent overcalls in a suit which you wanted to bid, double for penalties.

As South you hold

♠ K Q 10 x   ♡ A J 10 x   ◇ K   ♣ x x x x

The bidding has been

North	East	South	West
1 ◇	1 ♡	?	

You should double one heart for penalties. They are not going to make it. In fact, your profit should be substantial, even if North has a minimum opening bid.

B] If partner opens the bidding and the next hand overcalls at the two level in a suit you have well protected, don't bid two no trump, double instead and prepare to rake in the chips.

♠ A Q J   ♡ x x   ◇ J x x x   ♣ K 10 x x

Your partner opens with one heart and the next player overcalls with two clubs. Double for a certain profit. Even if your side can fulfill a three no trump contract, the profit from the double should provide adequate compensation.

c] The double of a low contract without the sign of
a trump trick is rarely contemplated by any
but the shrewdest operators. Analysis, however,
may prove such action to be surefire.

North, South vulnerable. East deals.

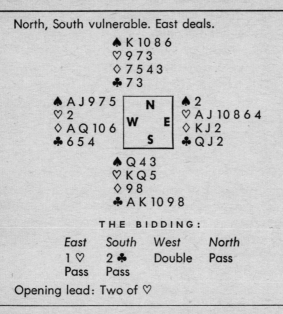

♠ K 10 8 6
♥ 9 7 3
♦ 7 5 4 3
♣ 7 3

♠ A J 9 7 5   ♠ 2
♥ 2   ♥ A J 10 8 6 4
♦ A Q 10 6   ♦ K J 2
♣ 6 5 4   ♣ Q J 2

♠ Q 4 3
♥ K Q 5
♦ 9 8
♣ A K 10 9 8

THE BIDDING:

East	South	West	North
1 ♥	2 ♣	Double	Pass
Pass	Pass		

Opening lead: Two of ♥

South chose to overcall the opening heart bid with
two clubs and the resulting punishment was out of all
proportion to the offense. West's action at this point
was sound. He doubled for penalties. West can count
with reasonable assurance on taking three tricks in
high cards and should beyond any doubt be able to
obtain a heart ruff, a total of four prospective tricks.
The opening bidder should be relied upon to produce
about three tricks in the play of the hand so that a
potential two trick set is in plain view. The 500 point
return is in excess of any game bonus that a non-
vulnerable team can score.

Without a brief glance into the future one might be
tempted to show the five card spade suit, in response to

partner's opening bid. This would be a drastic act in the present sequence. To show that suit would now require a bid at the level of two. If partner has no support for spades he may be obliged to bid three hearts. What then? West would be faced with no safe avenue of escape, and an almost certain loss would be incurred.

One must be extremely cautious in making "free bids" (that is, calls after an opponent has overcalled) at the level of two in any suit that is higher in rank than partner's suit. The reason is plain: partner will be forced to speak again at the nine trick level.

Against the doubled contract, the deuce of hearts was opened, won by the ace, and the singleton spade returned to establish the cross-ruff. The defense took in all three spade tricks, three heart tricks, and two diamonds, for an 800 point sting. And to make it all the more bitter for North and South, the maximum East and West contract was two hearts.

Warning:

You can double a two club or two diamond contract more or less "on suspicion," because even if the opponents should fulfill their contract it will not produce a game. However, a penalty double of two spades, three clubs, three diamonds, etc., must be made with greater assurance of success. Such doubles must be based on the expectation of defeating the contract at least two tricks. In other words, when the doubled contract will result in a game if fulfilled, the doubler should allow himself a one trick margin of error.

D] In calculating for a penalty double, count your tricks in a commonsense manner, and forget about points or the table of quick tricks.

Add the tricks you think you can take to the number you can expect from partner, allow one trick for margin of error, and let her go. Partner, of course, is to exercise a certain amount of discretion. If his hand is going to be a disappointment, from the defensive standpoint, he should not leave the double in. All doubles of low contracts should be regarded as cooperative.

Observe how South put simple arithmetic to use in the following hand to net a substantial profit for his side.

Neither vulnerable. North deals.

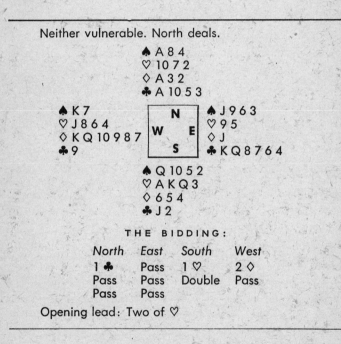

                    ♠ A 8 4
                    ♡ 10 7 2
                    ◇ A 3 2
                    ♣ A 10 5 3

    ♠ K 7   N   ♠ J 9 6 3
    ♡ J 8 6 4   W   E   ♡ 9 5
    ◇ K Q 10 9 8 7   S   ◇ J
    ♣ 9   ♣ K Q 8 7 6 4

                    ♠ Q 10 5 2
                    ♡ A K Q 3
                    ◇ 6 5 4
                    ♣ J 2

THE BIDDING:

North	East	South	West
1 ♣	Pass	1 ♡	2 ◇
Pass	Pass	Double	Pass
Pass	Pass		

Opening lead: Two of ♡

North opened the bidding on a hand that most players would prefer to pass. It is worth only 12 points. South chose to respond with one heart leaving room for his partner to show a spade suit at the one level. West overcalled with two diamonds and relieved North of the duty to speak. When it got back to South, he engaged in a little simple arithmetic. Since North had been unable to make a free rebid, it was highly improbable that his side could go game. Against the diamond contract, however, a number of tricks could be counted on. Since North had not supported hearts, it was not improbable that three tricks could be taken in that suit; the spade holding would, in conjunction with partner's holding, very probably produce a trick; and the opener could normally be counted upon to develop three defensive tricks. On this count, the contract could be set two tricks, so South doubled.

The deuce of hearts was opened. South won with the queen and returned a trump. North took with the ace and continued with a heart. North ruffed the fourth round, cashed the ace of clubs, and got out with a trump. This forced declarer to lead away from his king of spades. The total casualties were four heart tricks, two spades, a club, and a diamond. Down three! The 500 points were a handsome reward for North and South, who, it will be seen, could not reasonably have scored a game.

E] *Listen* to the bidding and revalue your own hand before counting defensive tricks.

For example, A Q (which the table lists as 1½ quick tricks) may be valued at two tricks for defensive purposes if the suit has been strongly bid on your right but should be counted as only one trick if the suit has been bid on the left. Similarly a guarded king may be treated as a full trick when the suit has been strongly bid on the right but would be assigned only a slight value if the suit has been bid on the left.

A maximum of two tricks should be counted in any

one suit, and if the suit is exceptionally long, only one trick should be counted for defensive purposes.

Holding four trumps in the adversely bid suit, even though they are small ones, count one trick for their nuisance value.

Be quick to double when short in partner's suit. Be cautious when holding as many as four of partner's suit.

F] *Listen* to the bidding and count your partner's defensive tricks as follows:

If he has opened the bidding with one of a suit—count on him for three tricks.

If he opens with one no trump—count on him for four tricks.

If he has made a takeout double—count on him for three tricks.

When partner has overcalled or given a single raise—count on him for at most one trick.

When partner has made a pre-emptive bid—do *not* count on him for any defensive tricks. Double solely on your own hand.

Penalty doubles don't always come up roses

Even experienced players with seasoned judgment will frequently be caught in the swing and keep doubling the opposition out of impulse rather than logic. The conviction is held that the enemy is floundering and it behooves the doubler to keep doubling everything in sight. Crafty players will frequently make capital of this psychological weakness by engaging in what is known as round robin bidding, that is, bidding in rapid succession suits which they do not really have, with the expectation of being doubled. After they have repeated the formula for several rounds of bidding, they arrive at long last at the suit in which they desire to play the hand, with the hope that the enemy will have gotten into the swing and continue to wield the mallet.

Both vulnerable. North deals.

♠ J 4
♡ K J 8 7 6
◇ none
♣ A Q 10 9 7 6

♠ 5   ♠ A 9 7 3 2
♡ A Q 10 9 4 3   **N**   ♡ none
◇ J 10 9 5   **W   E**   ◇ A K Q 7 4
♣ 5 3   **S**   ♣ K J 4

♠ K Q 10 8 6
♡ 5 2
◇ 8 6 3 2
♣ 8 2

THE BIDDING:

North	East	South	West
1 ♣	1 ♠	Double	2 ♡
Double	2 NT	Pass	Pass
Double	Pass	Pass	Pass

On the above hand, North elected to open the bidding with a club. While it lacks the honor strength for an orthodox bid, few players will today be found who would be willing to pass the hand. East chose the pussyfooting tactics of merely overcalling with one spade. He was reluctant to make a takeout double for fear that if he did so, he would be unable to cope with partner's probable bullish activity in hearts.

The trouble started with the double of one spade, which I am convinced was bad strategy on South's part. The trouble with doubles of low contracts when you have nothing but length in the adversely bid suit is that the hand many times does not play there and your partner will double some other contract depending upon you to take tricks which do not materialize in the play.

North's double of two hearts was natural and East rescued to two no trump with the diamond suit as a backbone. South passed as did West, and North made an impulse-double. Brief analysis would have shown that his partner could not have any strength in diamonds, else South would have doubled the two no trump contract, inasmuch as he is known to have the spades and partner had made it clear that he has the clubs and hearts. The contract was fulfilled with an overtrick.

North-South were caught in the swing.

Occasionally you should refrain from doubling the opponent in a close situation where the double may serve to locate certain strength for declarer that permits him to play the hand in an unnatural way. Where your trump holding is K 10 xx, for example, a double will warn declarer of the adverse distribution and may suggest to him that he play the trump suit unnaturally.

An even greater drain on the exchequer is caused by close doubles of slam contracts. There is not sufficient profit in them to compensate for the risk of affording declarer an occasional clue.

Sometimes in a highly competitive auction it is proper to double when you are quite certain that it would be disastrous for your partner to make any further bid, which he might be inclined to do if you failed to double.

Occasionally, you should take your partner out of a business double. These are the symptoms:

1] When your hand is not sound for defensive purpose—that is, you can take fewer tricks than partner expects from your bidding

2] You have freak distribution and are short in the suit doubled

3]   When you are confident that the double will not
prove sufficiently profitable and that more
points can be scored by going on to game or
slam.

South	West	North	East
1 ♠	2 ♡	Double	Pass
?			

♠ K Q 10 x x x   ♡ x   ◇ K J   ♣ Q J 10 x

With this hand you should not stand for the double.
Defensively speaking, your holding will prove a great
disappointment to partner. You cannot win three tricks,
which he expects.

One Final Warning:

Restraint and good judgment are called for whenever you contemplate rescuing partner from a contract
in which he has been doubled for penalties. Seldom
indeed is it profitable to use a no trump bid for rescue
purpose when you are extremely short in partner's suit,
although this hopeless maneuver appears to be employed all too frequently by many players whose experience should have taught them differently. In cases
where your honor strength is scattered, if your partner
is going to be badly off in his suit, you are apt to be
much worse off in no trump because of your inability
to utilize his hand. Bear in mind that if partner is
permitted to play at his own bid, he will be able to
avail himself of any high card strength that your
hand may contain, but in addition he will be able to
single in some of his low trumps by ruffing, an advantage which you will not enjoy if you run out to no
trump. It is a profitable maneuver only when partner
has solid top card strength in his long suit, all of which
can be cashed in.

North, South vulnerable. South deals.

```
                  ♠ Q 10 9 8 3 2
                  ♡ J 6 4
                  ◇ 5 3
                  ♣ 3 2
   ♠ 5 4            ┌─────────┐       ♠ A K J 7
   ♡ 9 8 7          │    N    │       ♡ Q 10 3 2
   ◇ Q 10 8 7 2     │  W   E  │       ◇ K J
   ♣ A J 7          │    S    │       ♣ Q 8 6
                    └─────────┘
                  ♠ 6
                  ♡ A K 5
                  ◇ A 9 6 4
                  ♣ K 10 9 5 4
```

THE BIDDING:

South	West	North	East
1 ♣	Pass	1 ♠	Pass
1 NT	Pass	Pass	Double
Pass	Pass	2 ♠	Double
2 NT	Double	3 ♠	Double
3 NT	Double	Pass	Pass
Pass			

Opening lead: Seven of ◇

It may be doubtful wisdom for me to publish the bidding that appears in the diagram above, but I can vouch for its authenticity. The damage was brutal and when the smoke had cleared away, South had managed to take three tricks and was poorer by 1,700 points and we hope much wiser for the experience.

After South opened with one club, North chose to respond with one spade. While this department does not see fit to endorse North's bid, we are not prepared to embark upon a crusade against such practice. Technically, it is a bit light. The text book requirement for a response at the level of one is six points. The North hand valued at spades counts five points, three in high cards and two for distribution. On North's behalf it may be pointed out, however, that his enterprising response might have yielded big dividends had South's hand been constructed somewhat differently. Interchange South's spades and diamonds and a game might have been scored as a result of North's sporting response.

South was now obliged to bid one no trump despite the singleton. North could see trouble brewing, so he elected to pass and take a short loss. East, whose previous pass had been very good strategy, now doubled and West cheerfully left it in. While North was willing to play one no trump undoubled, when the stakes were increased he could not stand for that contract at which his hand would be useless. His bid of two spades was plainly indicated and South should have taken his beating there. His rescue of two no trump when North had just escaped from one no trump doubled can only with unbridled charity be called indiscreet, and the subsequent rescue may perhaps best be described as incredible.

When North was asked why he had not persisted to four spades at which contract he could have salvaged 600 points, he replied quite aptly that he just couldn't cope with the prospect of having his partner bid four no trump.

4. *Preempts*

SOME PLAYERS ARE APT to think of the preemptive bid as a facet of deception. This is not a sound view. In making a preemptive bid, I don't have the feeling that I'm trying to fool anyone. My neighbor knows very well I have a weak hand, but if my action has any merit it is because of the crowding effect my bid has had upon him.

Players of the gay ninety era had a way of opening with a three bid on a long solid suit with a side ace or maybe two. Partner was expected to raise if he had a trick. This type of bidding fell by the wayside years ago. Now when partner has opened with a bid of three spades we are not expected to act unless we have three or four fast tricks—this is logical, for a non-vulnerable three spade bid is presumably an overbid of three tricks, and even in a vulnerable state the three bidder should be able to produce only seven tricks.

It should be apparent that the employment of this weapon with a partner of unknown quality is fraught with danger. She may be a product of the mauve decade, who will raise you with a lone trick. In unprobed situations of this kind perhaps it is best not to resort to the preemptive opening. You may resolve the situation either by opening with a shaded bid of one, or by passing with the expectation of coming into the bidding on a later round. I recognize that this is not ideal, but to borrow an expression from another field, "You can't win them all."

If you find this stranger opening with a bid of three keep a close eye on her (that is, her hand). You will soon discover the nature of her preemptive calls and adjust yourself to it on subsequent hands. Don't act impulsively and then justify your action or inaction by what "Goren says." You'd better try to find out what Mrs. Gotrocks says.

One other suggestion I wish to offer at this point: When, because of an opening preempt, a hotly competitive auction develops around the table, doubtful situations are bound to arise because of the unbalanced nature of the distributions. Observe this case:

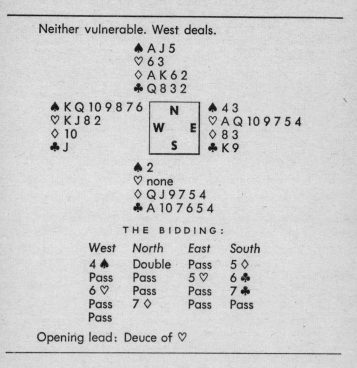

Neither vulnerable. West deals.

```
              ♠ A J 5
              ♡ 6 3
              ◇ A K 6 2
              ♣ Q 8 3 2
♠ K Q 10 9 8 7 6              ♠ 4 3
♡ K J 8 2         N           ♡ A Q 10 9 7 5 4
◇ 10          W     E         ◇ 8 3
♣ J              S            ♣ K 9
              ♠ 2
              ♡ none
              ◇ Q J 9 7 5 4
              ♣ A 10 7 6 5 4
```

THE BIDDING:

West	North	East	South
4 ♠	Double	Pass	5 ◇
Pass	Pass	5 ♡	6 ♣
6 ♡	Pass	Pass	7 ♣
Pass	7 ◇	Pass	Pass
Pass			

Opening lead: Deuce of ♡

Orthodox practices were thrown to the winds in both bidding and play in this deal. Note that in all such auctions, all reasonable doubts should be resolved in favor of aggressive action. The loss by bidding is apt to be less damaging than the loss involved in letting the op-

ponents play at their own price. An additional bid,
though it results in a set, may prove to be sound in-
surance.

West opened with four spades which North doubled
in a mild effort to increase the revenue. South's action
in bidding five diamonds meets with our approval.
When East entered the auction, South, on the theory
that he had more to gain than lose by bidding, went
on to six clubs. When North made a forcing pass (quite
unjustified in our view), South continued on his merry
way. He was to be bound, it seemed, only by the limita-
tions of the bidding scale.

West opened the deuce of hearts. South ruffed, extracted the trumps in two rounds and was faced with
the problem of how to handle the club suit. Were this
combination of cards presented to declarer as an abstract problem, the answer, right out of the pages of
the textbook, would be readily available. It would
be proper to lay down the ace. The suit can be picked
up in one of two ways: *1*] by dropping a singleton king;
or *2*] by finding the singleton jack to the left of the
ace. In this case the queen is played and when second
hand covers, the jack is crushed under the ace.

The play of the ace is superior because it succeeds
in two cases: When West has a singleton king and
also when East has a singleton king; whereas, leading
the queen through succeeds only when West has the
singleton jack.

On the flimsiest of evidence declarer decided to abandon percentages and play a hunch. On the basis of
the opening four spade bid he decided that West had
at least seven spades, and in view of the six heart
bid he mentally marked him with four of that suit.
When he showed up with one diamond, it was reasonable to assume that he had only one club. Was it the
king or the jack? For if it was neither there was no

hope. After a protracted bit of agonizing, South decided to play West for the jack. From the circumstance that East had bid for eleven tricks, he thought it more likely that East's club holding was K 9 rather than J 9. Then, too, there was the further consideration that if West held ♠ K Q 10 x x x x, ♡ K J x x, ◊ x, ♣ K it was too good for a preemptive bid.

Declarer led the queen of clubs from dummy, and East was helpless. If he ducked, declarer had no choice but to let it ride. If he covered, all came crashing down.

Here is another interesting case where both sides went to nearly the ultimate limit.

East-West vulnerable. West deals.

```
              ♠ A K Q 2
              ♡ none
              ◊ 10 7 6 4 3 2
              ♣ 8 7 4
  ♠ J                          ♠ none
  ♡ A Q 10 8 6 5      N        ♡ K J 9 7 4 3 2
  ◊ K J 9         W     E      ◊ Q 8 5
  ♣ K J 9             S        ♣ Q 10 2
              ♠ 10 9 8 7 6 5 4 3
              ♡ none
              ◊ A
              ♣ A 6 5 3
```

THE BIDDING:

West	North	East	South
1 ♡	Pass	4 ♡	4 ♠
5 ♡	5 ♠	6 ♡	Double
Pass	6 ♠	Pass	Pass
Double	Pass	Pass	Pass

Opening lead: Jack of ♠

The bidding proceeded along normal lines for the first round or two, and then suddenly went off on a tangent. East's preemptive raise to four hearts was quite orthodox. With little or no defense, the jump was calculated to bar a possibly irritating overcall in spades, against which East's holding would be altogether impotent. South, holding a freak of nature, was not to be shut out. West and North carried on the competition, and East bid six hearts, not with any hope of fulfilment, but rather as a sacrifice against five spades. South thought his two aces justification for doubling, but North decided that by this time the contest had degenerated into a game of roulette and considered that he had more to gain by bidding than by permitting the double to stand.

West, faced with a choice of unattractive leads, decided to open the jack of trumps. This proved to be a deadly salvo as far as declarer's hopes were concerned, for it apparently deprived dummy of one of the three entries necessary to establish the long diamond suit. Only if diamonds broke 3–3 could declarer bring in his ambitious contract; otherwise the loss of two club tricks could not be avoided, and even under the most favorable conditions three entries would be required.

A quick survey of the trump suit revealed that West's jack of spades was the only outstanding trump. The opportunity for an interesting gambit therefore presented itself. At the bargain price of one trick, declarer was able to purchase an additional entry to dummy. He ducked the jack of spades!

West shifted to a club, driving out declarer's ace. The ace of diamonds was cashed and a trump led to dummy's queen. A diamond was ruffed in the closed hand, and dummy was re-entered with the king of spades. When another diamond ruff dropped the king and queen, dummy's three diamonds became established, and the ace of spades was the final entry to dummy to permit declarer to discard his three small clubs.

Observe that if declarer takes the first trick he has no play for his contract.

Even the most astute opposition is at times rendered helpless by the proper and timely application of preemptive principles. When you realize that the enemy has an important message to get through, that is the time to jam their communications, as witness this hand.

East-West vulnerable. South deals.

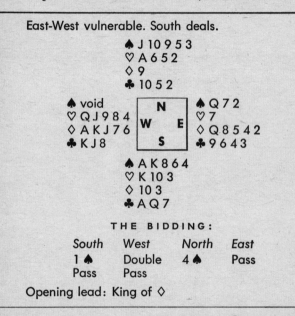

```
              ♠ J 10 9 5 3
              ♡ A 6 5 2
              ◊ 9
              ♣ 10 5 2
  ♠ void           N         ♠ Q 7 2
  ♡ Q J 9 8 4            E   ♡ 7
  ◊ A K J 7 6   W           ◊ Q 8 5 4 2
  ♣ K J 8           S       ♣ 9 6 4 3
              ♠ A K 8 6 4
              ♡ K 10 3
              ◊ 10 3
              ♣ A Q 7
```

THE BIDDING:

South	West	North	East
1 ♠	Double	4 ♠	Pass
Pass	Pass		

Opening lead: King of ◊

After South's opening bid West was faced with a mild problem. It was his desire to describe a strong hand and yet he might find it expedient to show both suits should the bidding develop in a mild manner. A mere overcall of two hearts would not do justice to the hand and might even result in failure to reach the best contract. After due consideration West elected to double.

North's preemptive raise to four spades was well

chosen. The enemy was trying to find a "spot" and to do so at the level of five would be extremely difficult. Despite partner's opening bid the chances were that the North-South defensive strength would not be very formidable. The best tactics seemed to be to place the pressure upon the adversaries to make the correct guess. East could take no action and West was up against it. He felt he was being talked out of something, but what could he do? Any bid by him would be a mere stab in the dark and might prove disastrous.

It will be noted that East and West could have made five diamonds but it would have required master minding of the first order to get there in the face of the barricade. This is one of the reasons many players dislike to make informative doubles with two suiters. Had West chosen to overcall with hearts he would be in a position where he might, if he felt so inclined, try five diamonds, hoping that one or the other might find a fit in partner's hand.

The king of diamonds was led and then West shifted to the queen of hearts. Declarer won with the king and tested the trump suit. When West showed out he ruffed a diamond in dummy and took the trump finesse, clearing the suit. A heart was led to the ace and a heart back went to West. The fourth round of hearts was led by West but declarer did not ruff. Instead he discarded the seven of clubs and the enemy was on lead, with no way to score another trick. The lead of a red card would permit a ruff in dummy and the discard of the queen of clubs in the closed hand and a club return would be into South's tenace.

For years the defensive jump overcall was employed to describe a big hand. Although it was a satisfactory device, occasions for its use were infrequent. It was discovered that the bid served a more useful purpose when exercised as a preemptive measure to describe a good suit but a weak hand. It represents a good lead-director for partner and occasionally paves the way for a profitable sacrifice.

Neither vulnerable. North deals.

```
                ♠ K J 4
                ♡ 7 6 3
                ◇ A K J 9 8
                ♣ 10 4
   ♠ 7 6 5          N          ♠ 8 3 2
   ♡ 5 4                       ♡ A K 10 9 8 2
   ◇ 7 6 5     W       E       ◇ 2
   ♣ A K 9 7 3        S        ♣ J 8 6
                ♠ A Q 10 9
                ♡ Q J
                ◇ Q 10 4 3
                ♣ Q 5 2
```

THE BIDDING:

North	East	South	West
1 ◇	2 ♡	2 ♠	Pass
3 ◇	Pass	3 NT	Pass
Pass	Pass		

Opening lead: King of ♣

North opened the bidding with one diamond and East threw a monkey wrench into the proceedings by his jump overcall of two hearts. It proved most effective in inhibiting North's effort to sign off subsequently.

South had a comfortable forcing response of two spades but North found his rebid anything but comfortable. He could not pass, and his rock bottom minimum opening bid discouraged a raise of partner's spades, so he chose the rebid that sounded the least encouraging, namely three diamonds. South chose to

gamble that partner had a heart honor by calling three
no trump, with a mental reservation against sticking it
out should he be greeted with a double.

The defense was both quick and devastating. West
opened the king of clubs to inspect the terrain and,
noting his partner's eight, shifted to a heart. East
rattled off the next six tricks and followed with the
jack of clubs through declarer to complete a 350 point
rout. Note that West's normal opening, without
East's jump overcall, would be the seven of clubs.

Among the more recent developments in contract
bridge, perhaps one of the most colorful is the "unusual no trump convention." It provides that where a
player makes a bid of any number of no trumps *which
could not possibly mean what it says*, then the no trump
bid is to be construed as a takeout double and partner
is expected to respond in his best minor suit. Suppose,
for example, opponents have bid an opening one spade
and a jump raise to three spades. If you now bid three
no trump over the three spade raise, it is highly unlikely that you can have the spade suit adequately
stopped.

The common sense of the situation is this: If a
player makes a takeout double of one major suit, it is
reasonable to suppose that he would like to hear his
partner respond in the other major. But where the
prospective doubler is not prepared for the other
major, he obtains the effect of doubling for a minor
suit response by using an unnatural overcall in no
trump.

This weapon is often effective both as a preemptive
device and also against an opponent's preemptive bid.
In fact, it is a bid usually made at high level where it is
difficult to bid both minors and let your partner make a
choice.

Both vulnerable. East deals.

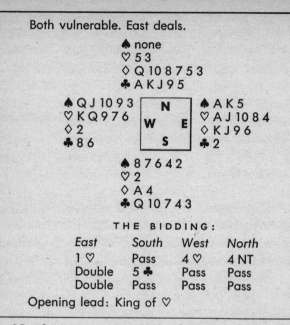

```
                    ♠ none
                    ♡ 5 3
                    ◇ Q 10 8 7 5 3
                    ♣ A K J 9 5
   ♠ Q J 10 9 3      ┌─────┐      ♠ A K 5
   ♡ K Q 9 7 6       │  N  │      ♡ A J 10 8 4
   ◇ 2          W  │     │  E    ◇ K J 9 6
   ♣ 8 6             │  S  │      ♣ 2
                    └─────┘
                    ♠ 8 7 6 4 2
                    ♡ 2
                    ◇ A 4
                    ♣ Q 10 7 4 3
```

THE BIDDING:

East	South	West	North
1 ♡	Pass	4 ♡	4 NT
Double	5 ♣	Pass	Pass
Double	Pass	Pass	Pass

Opening lead: King of ♡

North was convinced there was no defense to the heart game and felt a saving could be effected by a sacrifice bid in a minor suit. But which one? A bid of five diamonds might prove disastrous if South were short there.

North decided, therefore, to make partner pick the suit by a bid of four no trump. Obviously this was not a Blackwood call but served the purpose of a takeout double. However, there is a delicate inference flowing from North's bid. Inasmuch as he had made it impossible for partner to bid four spades, it must be that he is not interested in the other major and partner is asked to select his best minor suit. East doubled to show his strong defensive values, and after South chose clubs for the takeout, East repeated his double. Perhaps West should not have left it in, but we cannot find it in ourselves to criticize him.

East's four heart contract could have been de-

feated only through the unlikely opening lead of a
spade. Actually North and South would have to go
some to set five hearts. Although North intended his
bid as an effort to find a cheap sacrifice, South proceeded
to make the contract.

West opened the king of hearts and South ruffed
the continuation. Declarer drew trumps and then
played ace and another diamond. Although the suit
broke badly, he still had two trumps left with which to
ruff out East's holding and set up dummy.

The use of the unusual no trump is also a powerful
offensive weapon. It led to some strange ramifications
on this hand.

Both vulnerable. West deals.

```
                    ♠ J 6 3
                    ♡ Q 7 6
                    ◇ K 7 5 3
                    ♣ 9 7 2
    ♠ Q 10 9 7 4   ┌─────────┐   ♠ K 8 5 2
    ♡ A K 8        │    N    │   ♡ J 10 9 4 3 2
    ◇ A 9 8        │ W     E │   ◇ 2
    ♣ Q 4          │    S    │   ♣ 6 3
                   └─────────┘
                    ♠ A
                    ♡ 5
                    ◇ Q J 10 6 4
                    ♣ A K J 10 8 5
```

THE BIDDING:

West	North	East	South
1 ♠	Pass	2 ♠	2 NT
4 ♠	Pass	Pass	5 ♣
Double	Pass	Pass	Pass

Opening lead: King of ♡

West opened with one spade and East offered a single
raise. A takeout double was not available to South because of his shortage in hearts. The situation was made

to order for the unusual no trump requesting partner's best minor suit. West leaped to four spades, partly for obstructive purposes and partly with the hope of fulfilling contract. North took no action and when South proceeded to five clubs, West decided to double.

Perhaps North, at this point, should bid five diamonds. It is to be recalled that South offered his partner a choice of clubs and diamonds and North's preference for diamonds appears to be clear. In fact, North's failure to bid five diamonds is inexcusable. His partner had made precise use of the "unusual no trump" bid which is devised for exactly this situation. Unfortunately, North's opponents had no trouble interpreting South's no trump bid.

West opened the king of hearts. The appearance of the dummy and partner's deuce discouraged a continuation and West alertly shifted to the ace and another diamond. He properly concluded that South's unnatural no trump bid was based on at least five of each of the minors.

Admittedly, North and South were the victims of a bad break and brilliant defense, but a five diamond contract would have been invincible.

Preemptive and interference tactics sometimes backfire by presenting information to the opponents which they might not otherwise obtain.

Dogged persistence in interference bidding by defenders is many times apt to prove highly enlightening to declarer when he is confronted with involved problems of dummy management. This is especially true when declarer holds the lion's share of high cards and knows that defensive bidding must be based on distribution. What a help in planning the play of the hand. Observe how South in this hand gained the necessary clues from East's "operations."

North-South vulnerable. South deals.

```
                    ♠ 7 6 5
                    ♡ 8 5 3
                    ◇ Q 8 7 3
                    ♣ A J 10
    ♠ 3              ┌─────────┐      ♠ K J 10 9 8 4
    ♡ 10 4           │    N    │      ♡ Q J 9 7 2
    ◇ 5 4 2          │  W   E  │      ◇ none
    ♣ Q 8 7 6 5 4 2  │    S    │      ♣ K 9
                     └─────────┘
                    ♠ A Q 2
                    ♡ A K 6
                    ◇ A K J 10 9 6
                    ♣ 3
```

THE BIDDING:

South	West	North	East
2 ◇	Pass	3 ◇	4 ♠
4 NT	Pass	5 ◇	5 ♡
6 ◇	Pass	Pass	Pass

Opening lead: Three of ♠

South's two diamond bid and North's raise were fairly standard and East participated with a preemptive jump overcall of four spades. East had no offensive aspirations, but hoped to lay the foundation for a sacrifice if West could support that suit. However, his five heart bid seems somewhat futile and tends to provide declarer with a road map.

West's lead of the three of spades was an obvious singleton and it appeared that declarer must lose a spade and heart and go down to a one trick set. However, he saw a ray of hope if East had exactly a five card heart suit.

South played one round of trumps and temporarily abandoned the suit when East showed out. He led the ace and king of hearts and breathed a sigh of relief when West followed to the second round. He then cashed the ace of clubs and ruffed a club. He now played the king of diamonds, and a low diamond to the queen. On the lead of dummy's remaining club declarer let go a heart from his own hand and West, who is now known to have nothing but clubs, was in the lead. On the forced return declarer ruffed in dummy as he discarded the losing spade from his own hand.

Occasionally a prospective preempter should restrain himself for fear that a high level bid will prove to be more inhibiting to his side than to the opponents. Take note of South's highly imaginative maneuvering on this hand.

Neither side vulnerable. East deals.

♠ K 7 4 2
♡ 7
◇ A 9 6 4
♣ J 9 5 3

♠ Q 10 9 6 3	N	♠ J 8 5
♡ 3	W E	♡ 9 5
◇ J 8 5 2		◇ K 7
♣ 10 7 2	S	♣ A K Q 8 6 4

♠ A
♡ A K Q J 10 8 6 4 2
◇ Q 10 3
♣ none

THE ACTUAL BIDDING:

East	South	West	North
1 ♣	1 ◇	Pass	2 ◇
3 ♣	6 ♡	Pass	Pass
Double	Pass	Pass	Pass

Opening lead: Two of ♣

South's overcall of one diamond was highly unorthodox, will not be found in any of the approved texts, and does not receive the indorsement of this department. However, it was not made for the purpose of putting over a "psych," nor was it an attempt to impress the gallery of kibitzers with the quality of his showmanship. There was method to his madness.

Holding game in his own hand, the routine call would have been a cue bid of two clubs forcing to game. South felt, however, that the orthodox procedure might not enable him to find out if his partner had some diamond support, which is the only thing he needed to give him a play for slam. Moreover, he didn't need the ace of diamonds. The king-jack would make it a lay-down, and the king and several small ones would give him a chance. His partner made a voluntary raise to two diamonds, whereupon he contracted for six hearts, confident that he could hold his diamond losses to one trick. East, under the mistaken impression that South was shooting in the dark, indiscreetly doubled, and the contract was fulfilled with little effort.

It may be argued that in making a simple overcall, South subjected himself to the risk of having the hand passed out at one diamond. Of this there is no doubt. However, it will be observed that the risk is theoretical, rather than real. When one player holds a nine card suit and another opens the bidding, the cards will be found to be distributed in such a fashion as to make a pass-out at the one level extremely unlikely. Besides, we don't supply bidding rules for hands containing nine card suits.

5. *Slam Bidding*

"WHAT DO YOU THINK of the Blackwood (or Gerber) convention?" is a question that is thrown at me with monotonous regularity. Such a query cannot be answered in the abstract. Obviously there is nothing wrong with the convention itself, but there may be a great deal wrong with the manner in which it is handled by some players. The merits of the convention can hardly be treated soundly without reference to a specific holding. Tell me what you hold and I may be in a position to offer advice as to whether to employ the four no trump bid—or whether to abstain.

The fascination of Blackwood is so intense that many players cajole themselves into using the device even when their assets are not substantial enough to justify such action. There is a little bit of the district attorney in most bridge players, who find it difficult to resist the impulse to put their partners through the inquisition. "Come clean now, how many aces have you?" shouts the prospective D. A. The answer may place him in an untenable position. And only then he realizes that the time to have scanned the situation carefully was before embarking on the Blackwood wagon.

What I'm afraid of is not that the partnership hasn't enough aces but that we haven't enough tricks.

I like to emphasize that Blackwood should not be employed until it is determined that the partnership has a trick-taking potential of about twelve. Remember, Blackwood is not calculated to tell you how many tricks your side can win, it just tells you how many fast tricks can be taken by the enemy. Standard bidding methods are employed for the purpose of determining your trick-taking capacity. The point count gets you that far, then you check for aces to see if the opposition is apt to cash two aces against you.

But let us get on to some real life cases.

There are many instances in which a slam cannot be bid without the knowledge of partner's exact distribution. The only way to determine such facts is by natural methods, or what may be called picture bidding. In other words it is more vital to paint the picture of your hand as a whole rather than some specific feature of it. Take this hand, for example:

North, South vulnerable. North deals.

```
                    ♠ A 9 8 5 3
                    ♡ A Q
                    ♢ 10 6 5
                    ♣ A J 7
  ♠ K Q 6            ┌─────────┐        ♠ J 10 7 4 2
  ♡ J 2              │    N    │        ♡ 10 8 7 3
  ♢ 3 2              │ W     E │        ♢ 9 8 7
  ♣ K Q 10 9 8 5     │    S    │        ♣ 4
                     └─────────┘
                    ♠ Void
                    ♡ K 9 6 5 4
                    ♢ A K Q J 4
                    ♣ 6 3 2
```

THE BIDDING:

North	East	South	West
1 ♠	Pass	2 ♡	3 ♣
3 NT	Pass	4 ♢	Pass
4 ♡	Pass	5 ♢	Pass
6 ♢	Pass	Pass	Pass

Opening lead: King of ♣

On the second round of bidding North was faced with an immediate problem. Had the conditions of vulnerability been equal, North surely would have doubled the adverse club bid, and a juicy penalty would have been at hand. But since the opponents were not vulnerable, North was unwilling to accept a penalty which he feared might not amount to the value of a game and he bid three no trump. South's bid of four diamonds does not express a fear of no trump but is a distinct effort to go places. His bid of two hearts over one spade indicates at least ten points, and his bid over a game contract is therefore a clear indication of slam interest.

North elected to return to the major suit, and South decided to make one more slam try. He was morally certain that there was a heart loser in the hand inasmuch as North had not immediately supported the suit, but felt that the losing clubs could probably be disposed of on North's good spades if North could handle the club opening which seemed likely. In order to give a complete picture of his distribution, he bid five diamonds. This announces to his partner that he has five of each of the red suits.

This bid clarified the situation for North. He could visualize that his partner's diamonds must be solid and that if the hearts were not, one of them could be ruffed in dummy with a fairly high trump. As for the other three cards in South's hand, the black aces will take care of two of them; so North properly bid six diamonds. Only a club trick was lost to the opposition. It will be noted that a contract of six hearts would have failed because East held a heart trick, which disappeared when the hand was played in diamonds. And yet the partnership held all four aces at either contract.

Here is another case:

North-South vulnerable. South deals.

```
                    ♠ None
                    ♡ A K J 10 6 2
                    ◊ A K 10 6 3
                    ♣ 8 4
      ♠ K 5 4 3    ┌─────────┐   ♠ J 7
      ♡ 5 4 3      │    N    │   ♡ 9 8 7
      ◊ 8 5 4      │  W   E  │   ◊ Q J 9
      ♣ Q 7 2      │    S    │   ♣ J 10 9 6 3
                   └─────────┘
                    ♠ A Q 10 9 8 6 2
                    ♡ Q
                    ◊ 7 2
                    ♣ A K 5
```

THE ACTUAL BIDDING

South	West	North	East
1 ♠	Pass	2 ♡	Pass
3 ♠	Pass	4 ◊	Pass
4 NT	Pass	5 ♡	Pass
6 ♠	Pass	Pass	Pass

Opening lead: Two of ♣

In the early days of contract, possession of the spade suit became a great source of comfort, not only because of the advantage of rank enjoyed over the opposition, but because in any contest between obstinate partners the owner of the spades had the better prospect of getting in the last word. I recall a prayer that ran: "O Lord, deliver me from partners with spades." In more recent years, a newer menace has come into prominence, the player who asserts himself, at every opportunity, with his trusty four no trump call. But my heart really goes out to the player who, in his moment of trial, must face that type of player who comes armed with both spades and Blackwood, leaving his mate with no choice but to submit.

North was helpless before South's onslaught, and was left no chance to play the hand at six hearts. Such minor considerations as the king and jack of trumps gave South no concern when he learned that North had two aces. That there was a real danger of a shortage in spades in dummy should have been apparent when North bid two red suits, and North should have been given some choice in the matter. Had South abstained from the use of Blackwood in favor of merely rebidding his spade suit, North could have taken charge of the proceedings.

Fulfilment of a heart slam would have been routine, and in the absence of a trump lead North can win all thirteen tricks by ruffing out East's diamond stopper.

South's undistinguished bidding performance was matched by his manipulation of the dummy. West led the unbid suit and South won with the king of clubs. In an effort to get out the trumps, he led the ace and then the ten of spades, losing both the king and jack for a one trick set.

Despite South's abuse of Dame Nature, she had so distributed the cards as to permit fulfilment of the eccentric contract. Proper play after the ace of spades was the queen in the hope that both honors would bump. South contended that he was playing for a doubleton king of spades. Even if his wish were granted, he would be down on the contract, for if the king of spades fell on the second round there would be no way to pick up the guarded jack of trumps. The one hope was to find the jack doubleton, so that the queen of spades was the indicated play at trick three.

Slam Signals

What are the bids carrying slam implications? And when are you in slam territory? If the partnership has a combined total of 33 points, and a satisfactory fit, you are usually justified in embarking on a slam undertaking. But if you have an assured total of at least 34, you should not give partner a chance to quit. There are various ways to total the partnership assets but simple arithmetic will normally do the trick.

The problem may be approached (a) from the opening bidder's viewpoint, (b) from the responder's viewpoint.

(*a*) THE OPENING BIDDER'S VIEWPOINT

1] When the responder shows the equal of an opening bid:

Opener	Responder		Opener	Responder
1 ♡	2 NT	or	1 ♡	3 ♡

The responding hand is saying that he has from 13 to 16 points. This places the opening bidder in a position to approximate the combined assets by adding his points to the number partner has shown by his response.

If the total cannot approach 33, then the opener abandons hope of slam and is content to settle for game. But if the figure 33 is within reach, the opening bidder should exert some effort to determine if responder's jump was minimum or maximum.

2] Jump in a new suit (jump shift response):

An immediate jump shift by responder announces interest in a slam, inasmuch as the jump shift shows 19 points which assures a combined total of at least 32 (the opening bidder guarantees a minimum of 13 points).

3] Jump from one of a suit to three no trump:

This bid obviously implies slam possibilities. It shows from 16–18 high card points and completely even distribution. The responder therefore denies having any ruffing values.

(*b*) THE RESPONDER'S VIEWPOINT

1] In straight No Trump bidding it is merely a matter of simple arithmetic. Just add your points to your partner's and you have the combined partnership total.

If partner opens one no trump, he has 16–18.

If partner opens two no trump, he has 22–24.

If partner opens three no trump, he has 25–27.

Remember the pack contains 40 points.

26 points should produce game.

33–34 points should produce small slam.

37–38 points should produce grand slam.

2]   After a two demand Bid

If partner opens with a bid of two in a suit he announces that he can win at least nine tricks in his own hand. By adding these to the tricks you can produce in your own hand, you will determine the trick-taking capacity of the partnership.

♠ 10 7   ♡ K 2   ◇ A K 6 4 3   ♣ 8 7 5 2

Respond three diamonds to partner's opening bid of two hearts. If his rebid is three hearts, go on to six hearts. Your hand should be worth three tricks, and partner's bid promises nine tricks.

Note that there is no need to make a forcing jump bid to show strength over an opening bid of two. The opener has stated that the partnership cannot stop bidding short of game. Any positive response, therefore, alerts opener to the slam possibilities. Always take the big hands slowly so that the partnership can exchange all the facts. There is no danger of a pass below game, so why not keep the bidding at low levels.

Note that the opening two bidder does not have the same yardstick available to him because partner's response does not indicate a specified number of tricks. Where a fit has not been firmly established, the opener should explore further before making any positive commitment.

Both vulnerable. South deals.

```
                    ♠ Q J 9 8 6
                    ♡ K J 10 9
                    ◇ 6 4
                    ♣ 5 3
   ♠ K 7 3 2          ┌─────────┐        ♠ 10 4
   ♡ 6                │    N    │        ♡ 8 7 5 4 3
   ◇ Q J 10           │  W   E  │        ◇ 9 8 5 3 2
   ♣ J 9 8 7 4        │    S    │        ♣ 10
                      └─────────┘
                    ♠ A 5
                    ♡ A Q 2
                    ◇ A K 7
                    ♣ A K Q 6 2
```

THE ACTUAL BIDDING:

South	West	North	East
2 ♣	Pass	2 ♠	Pass
7 NT	Pass	Pass	Pass

This hand was submitted by South, asking for an indictment against North, who responded with two spades rather than two no trump. North's hand, he contended, did not justify a positive response, though he did acknowledge part of the blame on the basis of his undue aggressiveness.

Whether or not North should respond positively depends on your philosophy of the game. According to my lights, North has a good hand when partner makes a demand bid and it is my policy to bid two spades with that type of holding. The North hand is valued at 9 points, 7 in high cards, and 2 for distribution. The positive response may be made on a hand containing 7 points if it includes one quick (defensive) trick, or with 8 points, if it includes half a quick trick. The proviso that responder have a fairly good suit was complied with when North produced Q J 9 8 6.

South, for reasons best known to himself, proceeded with the assurance that North had a couple of kings and a queen. Curiously, even if North did have these cards, a contract of seven no trump would not necessarily be sound. Suppose, for example, North's response had been made on the following holding:

♠ K Q 6 4 2   ♡ K J 10   ◇ 9 6 4 2   ♣ 3

Even with this hand the odds are roughly two to one against fulfilling a grand slam contract. It would require a 3–3 break in spades which is very considerably against the odds.

After hearing the positive response of two spades, South should allow space for further conversation. Since the opening two bid is forcing to game, it is enough for him to bid merely two no trump at this point and await partner's further pleasure, intending ultimately to bid at least six no trump, or seven if partner indicates a solid spade suit or club support, in which case a grand slam in clubs would be likely.

3]   If the opening bidder jumps in a new suit

Opener	*Responder*
1 ◇	1 ♡
2 ♠	

he shows at least 20–21 points. This forces the bid to game and if the responder has an average hand or better, he should evince some interest in slam.

4]   A player holding the equivalent of an opening bid facing a partner who has opened the bidding and then jumped is an outstanding favorite for a slam.

Too often the potential slam hands go to the head, and otherwise cool and collected bidders fail to use the most elementary arithmetic in deciding where the hand might go and how to get it there.

Failure to make a simple addition and then the proper diagnosis on the following hand resulted in missing an easy six bid.

Both vulnerable. South deals.

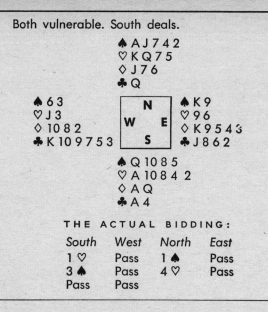

```
              ♠ A J 7 4 2
              ♡ K Q 7 5
              ◊ J 7 6
              ♣ Q
  ♠ 6 3              N          ♠ K 9
  ♡ J 3                        ♡ 9 6
  ◊ 10 8 2     W       E       ◊ K 9 5 4 3
  ♣ K 10 9 7 5 3    S          ♣ J 8 6 2
              ♠ Q 10 8 5
              ♡ A 10 8 4 2
              ◊ A Q
              ♣ A 4
```

THE ACTUAL BIDDING:

South	West	North	East
1 ♡	Pass	1 ♠	Pass
3 ♠	Pass	4 ♡	Pass
Pass	Pass		

North contended that his four heart bid was a slam try, and did full justice to his holding. We are not inclined to agree with him entirely. The four heart bid is not necessarily a slam try. It may merely be asking partner to take a choice of trump suits.

North should size up his own hand as follows: "I have a hand that is as good as an opening bid. My partner has opened the bidding and jumped. The hand fits well so there is a probable slam. Since my partner may have two losing diamonds, I shall pull my punches and bid only five hearts, which contract is surely safe."

Such a bid would have made it easy for South to bid the slam. As the bidding actually did progress. South was put to some pressure. My own feeling is that South might have been slightly more venturesome. He was well within himself on the jump to three spades and he might have made one more try. North is known to have a good hand, since if it were of the mediocre type, his best response would have been a simple raise to two hearts in preference to complicating matters with a spade bid in the meantime. South has all the important key cards, knows that the hand fits superbly, and I think might have taken his partner off the hook of his unduly cautious bid.

The Singleton in Slam Bidding

The shrewd contestant must recognize that many a slam is dependent, not so much upon aces, as upon distribution. The singleton may be just as important as the possession of aces and kings. Its value lies not only in its ruffing power, but also in its control of a side suit. It is comforting to know that even with both the ace and king, the adversaries can be limited to one trick in the suit.

Both vulnerable. North deals.

```
                  ♠ K Q 8 5
                  ♡ 9 4
                  ◊ K 10 7 6 4 3
                  ♣ 7
    ♠ 9 4            ┌─────────┐      ♠ 2
    ♡ Q 10 6 2       │    N    │      ♡ 8 7 3
    ◊ Q J 9 8        │  W   E  │      ◊ 5 2
    ♣ K J 6          │    S    │      ♣ A Q 10 9 5 4 3
                     └─────────┘
                  ♠ A J 10 7 6 3
                  ♡ A K J 5
                  ◊ A
                  ♣ 8 2
```

THE SUGGESTED BIDDING:

North	East	South	West
Pass	Pass	1 ♠	Pass
3 ♠	Pass	4 ♡	Pass
4 ♠	Pass	5 ◊	Pass
6 ♠	Pass	Pass	Pass

In this hand, for example, the slam depended upon North's possession of the singleton club. The suggested bidding is indicated in the diagram, but when I saw it in action, a player of wide experience, by the improvident use of the Blackwood convention, laid himself a perfect stymie, which he was not able to surmount. Just another case where the mere possession of aces and kings destroys the judgment of even the best players. In this case the singleton club was as good as king-queen in the suit, and yet there was no way to discover it, once South had uttered the fatal four no trump.

In third position, South opened with one spade and North, having previously passed, was justified in leaping to three. In the good old days, the rugged individualist, taking a chance that his partner had something in clubs, would straightway contract for slam with the South hand, a procedure, incidentally, which is not scorned by this commentator. But South, employing his trusty Blackwood weapon, asked for aces and North pleaded poverty. East, in order to suggest an eventual club lead, doubled the five club response. South, looking at two losing clubs, bid five spades and that was the final contract. As will be seen, twelve tricks were there to be raked in.

A Blackwood bid on the part of South was not indicated, because he did not need an ace from partner in order to reach for a slam. It would have been better strategy for South to have "told" instead of to have "asked." After the three spade bid, South should try four hearts, an ace showing bid. North, of course, will have to return to four spades. South now shows the ace of diamonds and North, knowing that the partnership can lose only one club trick, is in strategic position to contract for a slam.

Here is another instance in which high cards are not the only consideration.

Both vulnerable. South deals.

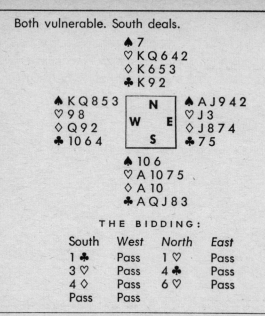

```
                  ♠ 7
                  ♡ K Q 6 4 2
                  ◇ K 6 5 3
                  ♣ K 9 2
  ♠ K Q 8 5 3      N      ♠ A J 9 4 2
  ♡ 9 8                   ♡ J 3
  ◇ Q 9 2      W     E    ◇ J 8 7 4
  ♣ 10 6 4         S      ♣ 7 5
                  ♠ 10 6
                  ♡ A 10 7 5
                  ◇ A 10
                  ♣ A Q J 8 3
```

THE BIDDING:

South	West	North	East
1 ♣	Pass	1 ♡	Pass
3 ♡	Pass	4 ♣	Pass
4 ◇	Pass	6 ♡	Pass
Pass	Pass		

When North's heart response is jumped by the opener, North should sense slam possibilities, and the diagnosis is based on the following considerations.

North himself holds a hand that is the equivalent of an opening bid if the king of clubs is regarded as promoted to the value of the ace by reason of partner's opening bid in that suit. His partner has opened the bidding and jumped. Since hearts are established as trumps, North can suggest the slam at this point by showing an ace. On the surface, the four club bid would announce possession of the ace; but since it is highly probable that opener has the ace of his own suit, he will understand that partner is attempting to designate the king. When South cooperates by showing the ace of diamonds, North is in a position to bid the slam on the basis of his singleton spade. South, of course, having two losers in that suit, is not in a position to assume the responsibility. In this hand the determining factor is not merely the aces, but the possession of the right singleton.

When a player names three suits and includes a jump bid in his sequence of calls, he promises a singleton or void in the fourth suit.

South holds:

♠ 10 x x   ♡ A K Q 10 x   ◇ x x   ♣ K J x

The bidding has proceeded:

South	North
1 ♡	2 ♣
2 ♡	2 ♠
3 ♣	4 ♡
?	

South bids six hearts, he knows that North has a singleton diamond because he bid three suits (clubs, spades and hearts) and also jumped the bid. North held: ♠ A K x x   ♡ J x x   ◇ x   ♣ A Q 10 x x

A leap beyond game, when nothing has previously been said about a suit which the opponents have bid, asks partner to bid a slam if he has no more than one loser in the adverse suit.

South:

♠ x x   ♡ K J 10 x x x   ◇ A Q 10 x   ♣ x

The bidding has proceeded:

North	East	South	West
1 ♡	2 ♣	3 ♡	Pass
3 ♠	Pass	4 ◇	Pass
5 ♡	Pass	?	

South should bid six hearts. North's five heart bid must be construed as requesting partner to bid a slam if he has no more than one club loser.

Cue Bidding as a Slam Technique

When a suit has been definitely established by the partnership as trump, the naming of other suits usually designates possession of controls—aces and kings—and evinces an interest in slam.

♠ A Q x   ♡ K Q 10 x x   ◇ A J 10   ♣ x x

South (opener) bids one heart, and North jumps to three hearts. Partner's response shows from 13–16 points. Opener's hand is worth 18 rebid points. If partner has a minimum raise, there will be no slam. If he has a raise containing 15 or 16, the slam may be there.

South shows his interest in slam by bidding three spades (a cue bid), announcing the ace of spades. If North counters by bidding four clubs, showing the ace of that suit, South bids four diamonds. If North should now bid five diamonds, it would show the king.

An interesting negative inference can sometimes be made, which is like a critic's comment on a play: "Revealing because of what it didn't say." Thus, failure to show an ace when there was a convenient opportunity to do so usually indicates the lack of that ace.

♠ x x   ♡ Q J x x x   ◇ A x   ♣ K Q J 10

Assume the bidding to have been

North	South
1 ♡	3 ♡
5 ♡	?

South should pass even though he has maximum jump raise of 16 points. Partner failed to show either black ace when it was convenient to do so, therefore must be presumed to lack both.

North's hand was:

♠ K Q x   ♡ A K 10 x x   ◇ K Q J   ♣ x x

The void suit is the delight as well as the bane of the slam bidder's existence. Where the void is held in a suit which has been bid by the enemy, it is a most valuable ingredient, easily communicated to partner. Where, however, it is in the suit in which partner has opened the bidding, it is usually a cause for concern and is almost inevitably a psychological barrier to the attainment of the ultimate.

The holder of the void must exercise delicacy in the choice of the methods to be employed for determining the possibilities of the hand. It is rarely indeed that the Blackwood convention is available to him. Blackwood is an asking bid and I think it will be agreed that it is pointless to ask a question when one does not know what to do with the answer. The number of aces held by partner is not the issue. Specific information as to which ones he holds is required.

Neither vulnerable. North deals.

```
              ♠ A 10 5
              ♡ A J 6
              ◊ 9 8 2
              ♣ K Q 10 2
  ♠ K Q 8 2      ┌─────┐     ♠ J 9 6 4 3
  ♡ 10 9 7 4     │  N  │     ♡ 8 3 2
  ◊ J            │ W E │     ◊ none
  ♣ A J 6 4      │  S  │     ♣ 9 8 7 5 3
                 └─────┘
              ♠ 7
              ♡ K Q 5
              ◊ A K Q 10 7 6 5 4 3
              ♣ none
```

THE BIDDING HAS PROCEEDED:

North	East	South	West
1 ♣	Pass	2 ◊	Pass
2 NT	Pass	3 ◊	Pass
3 ♠	Pass	4 ◊	Pass
4 ♡	Pass	7 ◊	Pass
Pass	Pass		

North opened with one club. South flashed the immediate slam signal by making a jump shift to two diamonds. North rebid two no trump to show a near minimum holding with a balanced distribution. South's rebid of three diamonds was proper. There was no necessity for jumping again. The jump shift slam signal had already been sounded and South should act on the assumption that it was heard by partner.

This call had the merit of economy and permitted North to show the ace of spades inexpensively. South again made things easy for partner by bidding only four diamonds. This served a dual purpose. It established, beyond doubt, the solidity of the diamonds and made it clear that South intended to play the final contract in that suit. Secondly, it made it easy for North to infer that his partner was affording him the opportunity to show another ace if he had one. This he did by bidding four hearts, and the seven diamond bid followed as a matter of course. A Blackwood call by South would have served no good purpose, for if North showed two aces South could not safely bid a grand slam inasmuch as one of the aces might be in the club suit.

On the surface it may appear that North was overly aggressive in opening the bidding and then showing two aces with a hand containing only slightly more than a bare minimum. This is a good example of partnership confidence. North was convinced that partner would not overestimate his strength. By his first rebid of two no trump, he had designated that he had a more or less limited opening. His subsequent ace showing bids could not, therefore, be construed as disclosing added values, but merely as identifying his aces. After all, one of his aces might have been in clubs, for which South would have no use. In other words, the ace of clubs in the North hand would have represented a duplication of values.

More on the Subject of Duplication

It is a good general principle of bidding that if you do not afford your partner the opportunity to show a certain feature then it follows that you have no interest in that feature. There are times when an otherwise glamorous card is plainly recognizable as worthless. Sometimes a delicate touch is required to determine that certain cards are without value.

Both sides vulnerable. South deals.

```
                    ♠ 6 2
                    ♡ A K 7 4 3
                    ◇ 5 3
                    ♣ A 9 5 2
        ♠ A 8          ┌─────────┐     ♠ 4 3
        ♡ 10 9 6       │    N    │     ♡ Q J 8 5 2
        ◇ 10 8 2       │  W   E  │     ◇ 9 7
        ♣ K Q 10 6 3   │    S    │     ♣ J 8 7 4
                       └─────────┘
                    ♠ K Q J 10 9 7 5
                    ♡ none
                    ◇ A K Q J 6 4
                    ♣ none
```

THE BIDDING:

South	West	North	East
6 ♠	Pass	7 ♠	Pass
Pass	Double	Pass	Pass
Pass			

Opening lead: King of ♣

The bidding is given as it actually occurred, but the recriminations between partners have not been included. North contended that when partner could open vulnerable with six spades, he surely had the right to raise once with three gilt edged high card tricks. South insisted that it couldn't be wrong for him to bid a slam when he had it laydown in his own hand, and that North should not have regarded South's bid as an invitation to go seven. Who was guilty?

I am afraid that North has no defense to the indictment. He reasoned that partner could take twelve tricks and he could take three. That adds up to fifteen. On that line of reasoning, he should have bid nine spades. Obviously, one of his aces is useless, because South would not have opened with a slam if he had two losers. Well, if one of the aces is useless, isn't it barely possible that the other one is useless too?

One thing is certain, the South hand contains only one loser, but the question arises in what suit is that loser? If it were in hearts or clubs, wouldn't South open with a two bid and then give his partner a chance to show his aces? The very fact that South did not afford North the opportunity to show either the ace of clubs or the ace of hearts makes it clear that he is not interested in either of them.

It follows logically, therefore, that South's only loser must be in trumps and since North cannot help out in that department, he should be content with the small slam bid. In fact, it has become a convention that an opening bid of five or six in a major suit calls for a raise for every high trump honor held. For example: Partner opens with five spades and you have the king-queen of spades and nothing else. You should bid seven, because you know he was counting on losing to both the king and queen of trumps and the rest of his hand must be solid.

Playing In The Right Suit

Critical losses at the bridge table are frequently incurred not by bidding too much or too little, but landing in the wrong contract. In the following hand, the key to the slam lay in selection of the proper trump suit.

Both vulnerable. South deals.

```
                    ♠ K Q J 10 4
                    ♡ Q
                    ◇ K Q 9 7
                    ♣ A 10 6
      ♠ 7 2          ┌─────────┐      ♠ 9 5 3
      ♡ K J 9 6 5    │    N    │      ♡ 10 8 7 2
      ◇ 6 4          │ W     E │      ◇ 5 3 2
      ♣ J 9 8 7      │    S    │      ♣ K Q 3
                     └─────────┘
                    ♠ A 8 6
                    ♡ A 4 3
                    ◇ A J 10 8
                    ♣ 5 4 2
```

THE BIDDING:

South	West	North	East
1 ◇	Pass	2 ♠	Pass
3 ♠	Pass	4 ♣	Double
Pass	Pass	4 ◇	Pass
4 ♡	Double	4 NT	Pass
5 ♠	Pass	7 ◇	Pass
Pass	Pass		

South opened with one diamond and North elected to flash the immediate slam signal with a jump shift to two spades. While South held a minimum hand he felt it expedient to give an immediate spade raise, since his minimum holding contained the ingredients essential to a slam (suit controls). He reasoned that if partner had slam aspirations with only one ace—or none—the hand must be rather solid.

North then showed the ace of clubs, which East doubled in order to suggest an opening lead in that suit. South felt in high time to register a sign-off and took occasion to do so by passing. North then bid four diamonds and South showed the ace of hearts. Inasmuch as this was the cheapest bid available at the moment, it was a less dramatic step than it might otherwise be. West doubled, merely to register his presence, and North now bid four no trump. It was quite evident in this sequence of calls that North was not making an effort to play the hand at no trump, and South responded, therefore, by showing three aces.

North then contracted for the grand slam in diamonds rather than spades, realizing that the five card spade suit would provide discards for any club losers South might hold. In the minor suit the taking of thirteen tricks was routine. At spades, eleven tricks was maximum.

Another source of trouble is the failure to offer a quick raise. Though the direct raise with near minimum values may result in our occasionally getting overboard, we find ourselves more often playing a spade hand at spades and not at hearts or no trump. Large adverse swings are thus avoided.

Both vulnerable. North deals.

```
              ♠ A J 9
              ♡ K Q 10 4
              ◇ 6 2
              ♣ K J 5 4
♠ 8 7 6 4        ┌─────┐       ♠ 3
♡ 8 5            │  N  │       ♡ J 9 7 3
◇ J 10 8 7     W │     │ E     ◇ Q 9 5 4
♣ 9 6 3          │  S  │       ♣ Q 10 8 2
                 └─────┘
              ♠ K Q 10 5 2
              ♡ A 6 2
              ◇ A K 3
              ♣ A 7
```

THE BIDDING:

North	East	South	West
1 ♣	Pass	2 ♠	Pass
2 NT	Pass	3 ◇	Pass
3 NT	Pass	4 NT	Pass
5 ◇	Pass	5 NT	Pass
6 ♡	Pass	7 NT	Pass
Pass	Pass		

In this hand, North's failure to support his partner's suit resulted in a staggering loss for his side. Having opened the North hand with one club, we would have offered partner an immediate raise of his spade take-out. North asserted that he feared to do this inasmuch as partner was apparently thinking in terms of slam, and that he wished to avoid any undue encouragement. We do not hold with this view. If partner had responded with one spade to our opening bid of a club we would have felt constrained to raise to two spades, having a shade over our minimum requirement, adequate trump support and a ruffing value. By the same token the raise should be offered as more descriptive of the type of hand when partner makes a jump shift.

South's bid of three diamonds was a maneuver made in the hope of eliciting further information and at this point it was highly reprehensible of North not to show a preference for spades. South then resorted to a Blackwood call (after a jump shift, a four no trump bid is looked upon as a Blackwood call even if it is a raise of partner's no trump bid) and after ascertaining that his partner had an ace and two kings contracted for a grand slam at no trump. When neither hearts nor clubs would break he lost the hand.

It was admittedly hard luck that he was unable to pick up either the jack of hearts or the queen of clubs, but at a contract of seven spades it would have been easy to ruff out South's small diamond for the thirteenth trick.

Playing It From the Right Side

There are two factors which appear to affect the clear vision of a vast majority of bridge players. One is the possession of 100 honors; the other is the holding of a six card suit. Each of these conditions is apt to in-

duce a declarer complex, and when they are both present, partner's chance of playing the hand is negligible
indeed.

Neither vulnerable. South deals.

```
              ♠ 9 5 3
              ♡ K 9 7
              ◇ 10 9 6
              ♣ A K Q 6
   ♠ 10 6          N          ♠ 8 2
   ♡ Q J 10 8             ♡ A 6 4 2
   ◇ Q 8 5 4   W      E    ◇ J 7 3
   ♣ 9 4 3          S       ♣ 10 8 5 2
              ♠ A K Q J 7 4
              ♡ 5 3
              ◇ A K 2
              ♣ J 7
```

THE BIDDING:

South	West	North	East
1 ♠	Pass	2 ♣	Pass
4 NT	Pass	5 ◇	Pass
6 ♠	Pass	Pass	Pass

Opening lead: Queen of ♡

South opened modestly enough with a call of one
spade, and when North responded with two clubs, he
had good reason to get excited. With a certain segment
of the population, excitement produces a uniform reac-
tion, namely, the utterance of those magic words "four
no trump." North dutifully responded showing one ace,
whereupon South contracted for a small slam in spades.
The unfortunate heart opening set the contract before
declarer obtained the lead. True enough, had hearts not
been opened or had the ace of hearts been favorably lo-
cated, the slam contract would have been fulfilled. But
no complaint of hard luck can be sympathetically
heard, when it could so easily have been prevented by
the exercise of a little thoughtfulness.

In view of his holding of two small hearts, South's selection of a Blackwood call was ill-chosen. He might have maneuvered the bidding in such a manner as to afford partner the opportunity to bid no trump. A jump shift to three diamonds might have served the purpose and could always be followed by a Blackwood bid if warranted. The important consideration is that his partner might have the king of hearts which would make it obligatory for North to become declarer, in order to avoid a lead through that card on the opening. If North is to be declarer, it must almost certainly be at no trump. He should, therefore, be given the opportunity to bid no trump first.

Moral:

Avoid the use of Blackwood when your hand contains a worthless doubleton or tripleton in an unbid suit.

Both vulnerable. South deals.

```
                    ♠ K Q 7 6 5
                    ♡ 8 5 3
                    ◇ 10 9 6
                    ♣ Q 10
    ♠ 10 4 2           N          ♠ 3
    ♡ Q 2                          ♡ J 10 7
    ◇ 7 3        W         E       ◇ A 8 5 4 2
    ♣ A 8 6 4 3 2      S          ♣ K J 9 7
                    ♠ A J 9 8
                    ♡ A K 9 6 4
                    ◇ K Q J
                    ♣ 5
```

THE ACTUAL BIDDING:

South	West	North	East
1 ♡	Pass	1 ♠	Pass
3 ♠	Pass	4 ♠	Pass
5 ♠	Pass	Pass	Pass

To be set one at a contract of five in a major suit which you have reached on your own power is equally devastating to the exchequer and the morale. There is nothing ignominious in being down one at a contract of six. At least the victim may take a certain pride in the display of virility that led to the loss. He meets a soldier's death with important issues at stake. But he who climbs to five hearts or spades with no one in pursuit, and there encamps, is in a most unenviable position; he finds no hope of glory, no pride in having dared.

Which brings us to the sad case of Mr. South, or perhaps I might more properly say the sad case of Mr. North, who had no voice at all in the shaping of his destiny.

It is at the first rebid that South got himself mentally involved. Under the impression that he was making an absolute force he jumped to three spades and North proceeded to four. South, slam concious all the while, suddenly reached the conclusion that he had not done his full duty by the hand and urged his partner to proceed with a bid of five spades. The invitation was respectfully declined but the damage had already been done. There was no way to avoid the loss of a diamond, a heart, and a club.

South had placed his partner in a position where he couldn't come out whole. If North passed the three spade bid he would miss a game, if he proceeded to game his partner was intent on getting him overboard. South's wiser rebid after the spade response was a leap to four spades. I am well aware of the common cry that will greet this statement. "But that would be a shutout." Would it? Could South, having opened the bidding with one heart and then jumped in spades, deny that he had a good hand? *A player who has once opened the bidding with a bid of one in a suit can never, thereafter, make a shutout bid.* In other words, there is no such thing as a shutout rebid.

There was a further danger in bidding only three

spades. North might not be able to carry on and a
game could be missed. Suppose for example, North had
responded with one spade holding,

♠ K x x x x   ♡ x x   ◇ x x x   ♣ Q x x

He would surely turn a deaf ear to partner's plea if
it came in the form of a raise to three spades.

Blackwood

And so, finally, we come to the great slam-going
conventions. I have put them last deliberately.

Easley Blackwood, the originator of the Blackwood
Convention, when asked in what percentage of slams he
considered that the four no trump convention could be
properly employed, expressed the doubt that the figure
would exceed twenty-five per cent. Novices, on the other
hand, seem to feel that the four no trump call is a pre-
requisite to contracting for slam.

The essential ingredients of a slam are: A good
trump suit, a good side suit for discards, distribution
and aces and kings. When you have ascertained most
of the pertinent facts and have reached the point where
your only concern is the *number* of aces and kings held
by partner, then it is time enough to resort to the convention. In other words Blackwood should be employed
usually at the end of the bidding rather than the be-
ginning.

The four no trump bidder is the captain of the team,
and he alone decides the final contract.

The only exception to this rule is where the bidding
has indicated that the partnership has all four aces.
The responder may under this circumstance use his
own judgment as to the final contract.

Either player may bid four no trump. The responses
are as follows:

> five clubs shows   —no aces or four aces
> five diamonds shows—one ace
> five hearts shows   —two aces
> five spades shows   —three aces

After he has found out about aces, the four no trump bidder may ask for kings by bidding five no trump.

The responder shows the number of kings in the same manner as he showed his aces.

Warning: The five no trump bid must not be made unless it has already been established that the partnership has all four aces.

A perfect Blackwood example:

Both sides vulnerable. South deals.

```
              ♠ Q 8 7 4
              ♡ A 9
              ◇ A 8 4 3
              ♣ K 6 2
   ♠ J            N         ♠ 10
   ♡ Q J 10 2              ♡ 7 6 5 4 3
   ◇ J 9 6 2   W     E     ◇ Q 10 7
   ♣ Q 7 5 4      S        ♣ J 10 9 8
              ♠ A K 9 6 5 3 2
              ♡ K 8
              ◇ K 5
              ♣ A 3
```

THE BIDDING:

South	West	North	East
1 ♠	Pass	3 ♠	Pass
4 NT	Pass	5 ♡	Pass
5 NT	Pass	6 ◇	Pass
7 NT	Pass	Pass	Pass

The South hand lends itself perfectly to Blackwood treatment. North's jump to three spades is just the right call. His hand is worth 15 dummy points, 14 in high cards, because the queen of trumps is promoted to the rank of king, and 1 for the doubleton.

After North's jump to three spades, it is evident that no spade trick will be lost. If partner has two aces and a king, thirteen tricks can be counted. South, therefore, makes the conventional bid of four no trump and North's response of five hearts denotes two aces. The five no trump bid asks for kings and North's response of six diamonds shows one king. Thirteen top card tricks can now be counted and declarer might just as well play the hand at no trump to guard against the remote possibility that East might have a void of some suit and be able to ruff the opening lead.

Gerber Convention

A response of four clubs over an opening bid of one, two or three no trump is artificial and is treated in the Blackwood manner as a request for aces. The responses are:

four diamonds shows—no aces or four aces
four hearts shows   —one ace
four spades shows   —two aces
four no trump shows—three aces

Where the four club bidder wants to learn about kings, he uses five clubs as the asking bid. The responses are similar to those showing aces.

In Conclusion

Here are a few final assorted tips concerning slam bidding:

Remember:

The Blackwood Convention was not devised for the purpose of getting to slams. Its purpose is to stay out of them!

Blackwood is an asking bid, and I think it will be

agreed that it is pointless to ask a question when one does not know what to do with the answer.

It is well to note that a jump from one spade to three should not be employed when a slam is in contemplation. A jump in a new suit is the proper procedure in such cases.

When a slam depends upon either one of two finesses, it is virtually mandatory for good players to bid it. The odds are three to one in favor of the declarer.

On a great many deals, situations develop for which the art of man has not been able to devise the perfect bidding method. In those cases one must place his faith in probabilities and when a slam is likely, he should pull himself up by his boot straps and utter the mystic words.

6. *"I Never Hold Any Cards"*

IN A MOST ENGAGING PREFACE to one of my early books (*Better Bridge for Better Players*) George Kaufman, one of the greatest wits among our playwrights, complained bitterly of the frequency with which the cut of the cards shut him out of the South seat. Referring to South's natural talents he observed, "South holds the most terrific cards. . . . There is a lucky fellow if ever I saw one. . . . That's why I never win!"

We have all heard the vast numbers of these anguished complainers, but unfortunately most of them are not as amusing as Mr. Kaufman.

Here are a few samples:

1] "When my partner holds a big hand, I always hold a bust."

2] "On those rare occasions when I am dealt an opening demand bid that unfortunate character across the table from me finds himself looking at a Yarborough."

3] "Look at the rock crushers those obnoxious opponents always seem to hold."

4] "I never win a finesse."

5] "We always seem to wind up in the wrong suit."

There are numerous other complaints of this character to which you have many times been a witness.

All of these sound like the lines of Alibi Ike. Let me give you a reasonable transcription of their true meanings.

1] "We had a game but I refused to respond to my partner's forcing bid."

2] "My partner told me he had very little, but I had such a powerful holding that I persisted to an unmakeable slam. Sure, we were off two tricks, but my hand looked so big it was irresistible."

3] "Our opponents bid and made a game because our defence was quite uninspired."

4] "That finesse was unnecessary. I forgot to count my tricks."

5] "We had a game but we didn't get to it because I refused to take a choice of my partner's two suits. How could I bid on such a hand? He'd have thought I was giving him a raise."

Of course there is luck, but in my whole experience I've never seen it affect the year-in, year-out success of good bridge players. Most players to be sure run into an occasional bad streak—but if you are patient, inevitably the pendulum swings, and eventually it all comes back to you with interest. No, the consistent loser is the one who plays the single-handed game.

Strangely enough, this unlucky fellow is often a reasonably good card player and handles his dummies well. He simply can't be convinced that bridge is a partnership game. He bids only his own hand. When he holds a big hand he overbids and when he holds a mediocre hand he crawls into his shell.

There is one phase of bridge in which the vision of a great many players is somewhat less than 20–20, and that is the handling of the takeout double. Somehow the doubler's partner never seems quite able to visualize doubler's strength, while the doubler is rarely able to visualize his partner's weakness. One of the reasons for this blind spot is that takeout doubles vary considerably in strength. Only the doubler's second bid reveals whether his holding is minimum or maximum, loaded with high cards or distributional.

North, South vulnerable. South deals.

♠ 6 4 3
♡ Q 9 2
♢ Q 7 6
♣ J 5 4 2

♠ A Q J 8　　　　　　♠ 10 9 7 2
♡ K J 10 4　　N　　♡ 8 6 5 3
♢ 8 5　　W　　E　♢ 10 2
♣ K 7 3　　　S　　♣ Q 9 8

♠ K 5
♡ A 7
♢ A K J 9 4 3
♣ A 10 6

THE BIDDING:

South	West	North	East
1 ♢	Double	Pass	1 ♠
Double	2 ♠	Pass	Pass
2 NT	Pass	3 NT	Pass
Pass	Pass		

Opening lead: Eight of ♢

In this hand North picked up what looked like a handful of mud but shrewdly assayed it as gold.

West's double of the opening diamond bid was normal, and East responded with the best suit he had. South's double of the spade bid was of course for a takeout and is the indicated procedure to describe a powerful hand in this situation. A mere rebid of two diamonds would be grossly inadequate, and a jump to three diamonds would give no indication of South's distributed values. When West interfered with a two spade bid,

North was glad to be relieved of the duty to bid. But South was not yet ready to retire and tried once more with a bid of two no trump. North, who up to this point had taken a dim view of the proceedings, underwent a sudden change of heart and raised to three no trump, a bit of enterprise which we admire.

There was little doubt that South held a very powerful hand, for a sound player when vulnerable will not compete so vigorously for a mere part score against nonvulnerable adversaries, particularly with a silent partner. North sensed that South's aggressiveness was based to some extent on a long diamond suit, which his own queen would surely solidify. He decided that his partner's hand in trick taking potential was not far from the equal of an opening two no trump bid, so that with five points he chose to risk a game contract.

West, fearful of losing a trick by making an aggressive lead, opened the eight of diamonds. Declarer had eight winners off the top and was able to establish a ninth trick by leading towards the queen of hearts.

It is a weakness of a great many players that they form an early opinion about a hand and are unable to change it as the bidding develops.

Frequently a hand starts out with brilliant prospects, but when the bidding developments show that partner is not fond of either of your suits and you are unable to support his, what promised to be a breadwinner may prove to be just a deduction.

By the same token, you may pick up a hand with a few scattered pictures and no particular distribution, and you find it difficult to manifest interest in the proceedings. A round or two later the bidding may have convinced you that you have a card or two that may prove to be the missing links, and you promptly collect your wandering thoughts.

Neither vulnerable. North deals.

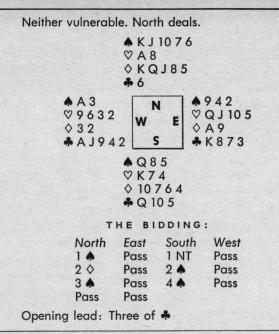

♠ K J 10 7 6
♡ A 8
◇ K Q J 8 5
♣ 6

♠ A 3
♡ 9 6 3 2
◇ 3 2
♣ A J 9 4 2

♠ 9 4 2
♡ Q J 10 5
◇ A 9
♣ K 8 7 3

♠ Q 8 5
♡ K 7 4
◇ 10 7 6 4
♣ Q 10 5

THE BIDDING:

North	East	South	West
1 ♠	Pass	1 NT	Pass
2 ◇	Pass	2 ♠	Pass
3 ♠	Pass	4 ♠	Pass
Pass	Pass		

Opening lead: Three of ♣

To the opening bid of one spade South responded with one no trump. Though he held normal trump support, the distribution of the hand was so barren that it was wiser not to increase the contract. North's rebid was naturally two diamonds, and at this point many players would be tempted to pass on the ground that "I like diamonds better than I do spades and have already told the strength of my hand."

I am inclined to believe that such reasoning would be superficial. Actually, the complexion of this hand has now changed. We are certain that North has five spades and four or five diamonds. If North had only four cards suits, he would have passed one no trump, or if his hand were sufficiently strong he would raise to two no trump. Rather than definitely consign this hand to a part score, I would suggest affording partner one more chance by returning to two spades.

Actually, South's preference is for diamonds, but since he is convinced that partner has five spades, the preference with three to the queen is not objectionable. North then decided that there was a chance for game, which he coaxed partner to bid by going to three spades.

South decided to take the gamble, hoping that the king of hearts would prove to be the key card. He well realized that if North had a singleton heart instead of club, his king might not be a vital card, but he was willing to take the chance and was rewarded for his enterprise when the hand proved to be a laydown.

It is not surprising that some players should be unable to make an accurate appraisal of hands that contain a wealth of high cards. But it is interesting to observe how many there are who have not yet picked up the knack of recognizing what really is zero. I have in mind principally the North of the next hand.

North, South vulnerable. East deals.

```
                 ♠ 10 8 6 4
                 ♡ Q 10 8
                 ◇ 10 9 6 5
                 ♣ 7 5
  ♠ J 9 5 3    ┌─────────┐   ♠ A K 7 2
  ♡ 7 6 5 2    │    N    │   ♡ 3
  ◇ J 2        │  W   E  │   ◇ K 8 7 4 3
  ♣ K J 4      │    S    │   ♣ Q 9 2
               └─────────┘
                 ♠ Q
                 ♡ A K J 9 4
                 ◇ A Q
                 ♣ A 10 8 6 3
```

THE ACTUAL BIDDING:

East	South	West	North
1 ◇	Double	Pass	1 ♠
Pass	3 ♡	Pass	Pass
Pass			

Opening lead: Jack of ◇

The opening of one diamond was doubled by South, and North dutifully responded with one spade. South then jumped to three hearts, and North passed with the comment, "Partner, I couldn't raise you. I knew you had a very good hand, but I had nothing."

South's letdown when the dummy was spread did not interfere with his routine taking of eleven tricks. For North to say that he had nothing indicates a refusal to look at his cards. That the queen of hearts was a certain trick there could be no doubt, and to see that partner would probably be able to ruff a club in dummy required no clairvoyance. Any hand that will develop two tricks cannot be regarded as hay when partner has doubled and jumped. North should have raised to four hearts without looking upon himself as a daring young man.

The suggestion that South should have bid four hearts himself is unsound because North might very well have been short in that suit, in which case such a contract would have little chance for success. The double by South is proper procedure, because if partner is short in hearts and long in clubs, a game in the minor suit is very probable.

South's statement that his jump to three hearts was an absolute force is not entirely correct. A jump shift following a takeout double is about ninety-eight per cent forcing, but if partner has nothing he may pass. However, at the slightest provocation responder should take action. Possession of any trick-taking probability constitutes such provocation.

Permit me to reiterate what I consider a sound principle of bidding strategy: When your partner has made a takeout double, all doubts should be resolved in favor of aggressive action. That is to say, when in doubt, *bid*.

Despite the proven accuracy of the point count method of hand valuation, it is not to be assumed that this yardstick will act as a substitute for individual resourcefulness. That cards may have rising as well as diminishing values, depending upon bidding developments, is a well established theory. An ear closely attuned to the bidding will frequently make it clear that a certain king is useless, while another king may be an assured trick.

Both vulnerable. South deals.

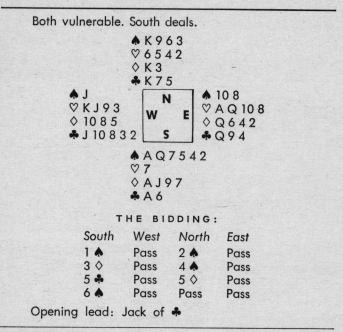

```
                ♠ K 9 6 3
                ♡ 6 5 4 2
                ◇ K 3
                ♣ K 7 5
  ♠ J                          ♠ 10 8
  ♡ K J 9 3         N          ♡ A Q 10 8
  ◇ 10 8 5       W     E       ◇ Q 6 4 2
  ♣ J 10 8 3 2      S          ♣ Q 9 4
                ♠ A Q 7 5 4 2
                ♡ 7
                ◇ A J 9 7
                ♣ A 6
```

THE BIDDING:

South	West	North	East
1 ♠	Pass	2 ♠	Pass
3 ◇	Pass	4 ♠	Pass
5 ♣	Pass	5 ◇	Pass
6 ♠	Pass	Pass	Pass

Opening lead: Jack of ♣

When North picked up his hand he saw nothing to emote over—three kings, a holding which could conceivably produce no tricks if fate decided to be perverse. But as the bidding developed he learned that he had, among other things, the equivalent of three aces, and by the third round of bidding was convinced that he held a powerful hand. This is a perfect example of the importance of revaluing hands as the bidding progresses. This is the heart of winning partnership bidding.

To the opening bid of one spade North decided to give a single raise, though there is some question whether the hand is not a shade too strong for such a response. On the whole, it is probably wise to choose a conservative path for the first response, especially when there is no logical way to indicate precisely what the strength of the hand is. Wouldn't it be helpful if we could bid two and a half spades on North's hand! South, of course, immediately realized that there was a game in the hand, but if North happened to have a maximum raise and in the right places, there even might be a slam. If North's values happened to be in hearts there would be no hope, but if they happened to be in the minor suits prosperity might be just around the corner. At any rate, there was no harm in bidding three diamonds, which was a one round force. North now indicated that he had a good raise by going to four spades.

It now appeared to South that five was safe; so he made one more try by showing the ace of clubs. You see what this did to North's hand: It converted every one of his honor cards to the equivalent of an ace. He was inclined to bid the slam himself, because it was inconceivable that South could do all this bidding with two losing hearts. However, he decided to show the king of diamonds, and South took the leap himself, feeling that at worst the slam would depend on some sort of finesse in the diamond suit. Actually, it turned out to be a laydown when it developed that he could easily ruff out his diamond losers.

Taking the Heat Off Partner

Generally speaking, a player who has previously passed should feel at liberty to take more aggressive action than his hand would otherwise call for.

Both vulnerable. South deals.

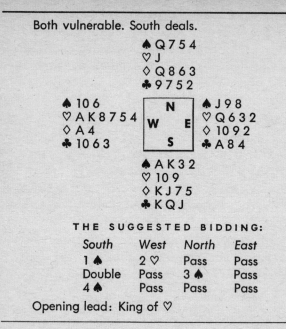

♠ Q 7 5 4
♡ J
◇ Q 8 6 3
♣ 9 7 5 2

♠ 10 6
♡ A K 8 7 5 4
◇ A 4
♣ 10 6 3

♠ J 9 8
♡ Q 6 3 2
◇ 10 9 2
♣ A 8 4

♠ A K 3 2
♡ 10 9
◇ K J 7 5
♣ K Q J

THE SUGGESTED BIDDING:

South	West	North	East
1 ♠	2 ♡	Pass	Pass
Double	Pass	3 ♠	Pass
4 ♠	Pass	Pass	Pass

Opening lead: King of ♡

North had nothing to cheer about when the cards were distributed. There was slight comfort, however, in the fact that partner had opened with a spade. When West overcalled with two hearts, North decided to take no action, but South quite properly felt that his hand was too good to give up the fight so soon and doubled for a takeout. If partner did not like spades, he might have something in clubs or diamonds with which to carry on the contest. However, North had formed an opinion about his hand that was not subject to change and in the actual bidding merely returned to two spades. South was obliged to give up the ghost and an easy game was missed.

In the post-mortem discussions, South contended that North should have given an immediate raise to two spades, since he had good trump support and a single-ton. To this view we do not subscribe. North's pass on the first round is good strategy. Had West passed, there would have been no doubt of North's obligation to keep the bidding open, but with an intervening bid, North did not have sufficient values for voluntary action. It is seldom good policy to make free bids when distribution is your only excuse.

When, however, South showed great strength by forcing partner to bid at this comparatively high level, North should have changed his mind about the value of his holding. The mere return to two spades might announce a hand with no values whatever, but merely the ability to play spades.

His proper bid at this point was three spades, which would say, "Partner, remember I passed the first time, refusing to give you a raise, therefore my hand was not worth one, but I have a hand that was nearly worth a raise. Use your own discretion."

Both vulnerable. East deals.

```
              ♠ A Q 10 9 8 6
              ♡ A K J 5 3 2
              ◇ A
              ♣ none
  ♠ 3 2                        ♠ K 5
  ♡ 7 4          N             ♡ Q 8 6
  ◇ Q J 10 3   W   E           ◇ K 9 8 7 6 4
  ♣ K 10 8 7 4     S           ♣ A Q
              ♠ J 7 4
              ♡ 10 9
              ◇ 5 2
              ♣ J 9 6 5 3 2
```

THE BIDDING:

East	South	West	North
1 ◇	Pass	2 ◇	3 ◇
4 ◇	Pass	Pass	5 ◇
Pass	6 ♣	Pass	6 ◇
Double	Pass	Pass	Redouble
Pass	6 ♠	Pass	Pass
Double	Pass	Pass	Redouble
Pass	Pass	Pass	

The cue bid of the opponent's suit is very often an effective way to get your partner to speak with an indifferent hand. However, when his holding is very weak, it may be necessary to repeat your message several times before it produces any effect.

The first round of bidding was strictly textbook material. When it got around to North, he took an oath to play this hand for no less than a slam in one of his suits but realized it would be vital to have partner decide which of the two majors would be the better vehicle. The proper procedure was the cue bid in opponents' suit, which was forcing to game regardless of how feeble South might be. East decided to jam things up a bit by bidding four diamonds, for which he gained South's everlasting gratitude. It was pleasant to be relieved of the obligation to bid, and he was thankful that the storm had passed.

North was determined to make his partner speak at any price and repeated the cue bid. East relaxed, and South did his duty by calling six clubs. This suited West too well to disturb, and it was back to North again. What he wished to say was, "No, partner, that is not the suit. Please try another one, either hearts or spades. I don't care which, but you must like one better than the other. Please, don't be afraid to speak up. It will hurt for only a minute." East by this time resented North's holding the middle of the stage and entered the auction with a resounding double. South again refused to budge. "I know that partner of mine has gone out of his mind," he said to himself, "but he got into it. Let him get himself out."

North by this time was getting out of patience with South's stubborn refusal to speak, but he had one more weapon at his disposal. He redoubled. This would have been no time for South to misunderstand. At his wit's end, he did at long last bid the better of his two suits, spades. East doubled and North went whole hog and redoubled.

Since the heart suit could be established by ruffing just once in the South hand, only one trick was lost to the king of spades. A tidy profit.

Misfits

A great part of the efforts of most bridge writers (including myself) is devoted to expounding methods for the handling of rock crushers. I wonder whether this is sound policy. True, we'd all rather be harbingers of good news; but misfits, like the poor, are always with us and unless one acquaints himself with the most effective means of handling these derelict members, a distinct curtailment of revenue is apt to be noticed. It is no trick to survive a period of good times but one must learn to take care of himself in a depression. Occasionally a misfit will respond to sympathetic treatment, as witness the result of well coordinated efforts on the part of North and South in this hand.

Both vulnerable. North deals.

```
                 ♠ A J 5 3 2
                 ♡ J 10
                 ◇ A K 7 5 4 2
                 ♣ none
   ♠ K 10 9 8         N        ♠ Q 6 4
   ♡ K 6                       ♡ Q 5 3
   ◇ J 9 3      W        E     ◇ Q 10
   ♣ Q 8 5 2         S        ♣ A 10 9 6 3
                 ♠ 7
                 ♡ A 9 8 7 4 2
                 ◇ 8 6
                 ♣ K J 7 4
```

THE BIDDING:

North	East	South	West
1 ◇	Pass	1 ♡	Pass
1 ♠	Pass	2 ♡	Pass
2 ♠	Pass	3 ♣	Pass
3 ♡	Pass	4 ♡	Pass
Pass	Pass		

Opening lead: Two of ♣

The first two rounds of bidding were according to all approved texts. North opened with the longer diamond suit and then rebid one spade. South, liking neither diamonds nor spades, was surely justified in rebidding his six card heart suit, and North then rebid the spades. This latter bid is very enlightening. The rebid of the spades unsupported by partner indicates a five card suit. Why then were diamonds bid first? The answer is plain. North must have more of them, which would indicate that he held six diamonds and five spades. With five of each, the orthodox bid would have been a spade first.

On the surface, it would seem, therefore, that South should return to diamonds, in which the partnership is known to have eight trumps. South's bid of three clubs however, was well chosen. He knows that in hearts and clubs North has only two cards. If he has one of each, he will naturally return to three diamonds, which South will pass; similarly, if he has two clubs. But if he happens to have two hearts and no clubs, he might be induced to give belated heart support, especially if he has an honor. This is what North actually did. In bidding three hearts he was not so much contemplating arrival at game as he was the finding of a safe port in which to weather the impending storm. However, South somewhat unsoundly gambled it out at four hearts and with careful play and a little help from the opposition was able to fulfill contract.

He permitted the opening lead of the deuce of clubs to go to the ace and when a trump was returned, he ducked. The defense could then find no way to take more than three tricks.

Locating the proper contract at which to play a hand sometimes presents difficulties to even the most experienced players. When the choice lies between two suits, almost invariably you should try to determine in which suit the partnership has the greatest number of trumps and select that suit, even though you personally do not prefer it. It is strange to observe how many players are unwilling to look beyond their own thirteen cards in selecting a trump suit.

"Partner, it made no difference to me, I had the same number of each," is frequently heard, without consideration for the question, "How many of each has my partner?"

If your partner bids hearts first and spades later, and you have three small trumps of each, it is your duty to return to hearts even though you dislike to increase the contract, because you should know that your partner has more hearts than spades. The following hand goes one step farther.

Neither vulnerable. South deals.

```
                 ♠ K 7 5
                 ♡ J 6
                 ◇ Q 10 2
                 ♣ A Q 6 5 3
      ♠ J 10 9 3     ┌─────────┐    ♠ 8 6
      ♡ A 2          │    N    │    ♡ 10 9 4
      ◇ K 8 7 6 4    │  W   E  │    ◇ A J 9 3
      ♣ K 9          │    S    │    ♣ J 10 8 4
                     └─────────┘
                 ♠ A Q 4 2
                 ♡ K Q 8 7 5 3
                 ◇ 5
                 ♣ 7 2
```

THE SUGGESTED BIDDING:

South	West	North	East
1 ♡	Pass	2 ♣	Pass
2 ♡	Pass	2 NT	Pass
3 ♠	Pass	4 ♡	Pass
Pass	Pass		

South opened the bidding with one heart, and North responded with two clubs. South bid two hearts and North, having virtually an opening bid, decided to move toward a game by bidding two no trump.

South, of course, was not pleased with the no trump idea and bid three spades. West passed, and North was faced with the problem which caused considerable trouble for the players who held this hand. Some of them stubbornly persisted to three no trump, and South, exhausted by his effort to warn partner away from no trump, gave up.

How this contract failed is quite apparent. Others, quite properly deciding that this hand had to play at game and liking spades so much better than hearts, took their partner to four spades. The diamond opening and the diamond return brought the declarer down to three trumps, and he was unable to manage the hand from here in. With the opponents having more trumps than himself, the hand collapsed.

North's vision had not been keen. The bidding shows plainly that South has six hearts and only four spades. Whenever the opener bids one suit twice before showing the other, in the vast majority of cases it shows that he has six of the first bid suit and only four of the second. If the holding were six and five, the six card suit would be bid first, but the five card suit would be shown at the next opportunity. It should have been clear to North therefore, that the partnership owned eight hearts and only seven spades, and he should have returned to his partner's first suit.

The question, "What is normal trump support?" is not one that may be answered in a phrase. The requirements vary with conditions, but a partnership should, as a rule, avoid reaching a game contract in a trump suit of which they hold less than eight cards between them. The standard texts provide that normal trump support for a single raise is Q x x or x x x x. In other words, one of the high trump honors is regarded as the equal of two small ones. So that occasionally opener may find himself playing a suit contract with only seven trumps, but in that case the dummy will have a high honor. The normal trump support indicated above allows that opener may have a four card suit.

If opener by his rebid has shown a good five card suit, responder may support if his hand is otherwise suitable, with x x x or Q x, and if opener has bid the suit three times without support from partner, a six card suit is indicated, and the raise may be made with two small trumps or the lone queen.

Both vulnerable. East deals.

```
              ♠ 5 3
              ♡ A K J 8 7 4
              ◇ A 10 4
              ♣ 7 5
♠ A K Q 9        N        ♠ J 10 8 2
♡ 9 6       W       E     ♡ 5 3 2
◇ 8 6 2          S        ◇ Q 7
♣ A 10 8 4               ♣ J 9 6 3
              ♠ 7 6 4
              ♡ Q 10
              ◇ K J 9 5 3
              ♣ K Q 2
```

THE SUGGESTED BIDDING:

East	South	West	North
Pass	Pass	1 ♠	2 ♡
Pass	3 ♡	Pass	4 ♡
Pass	Pass	Pass	

When I saw the above hand played, South actually bid three diamonds over his partner's two heart bid. This was a very ill-chosen call. First, because North is not obliged to respond to this change of suit. North is not the opening bidder and is, therefore, not subject to the "new suit forcing" rule. He is at liberty to check out at any time that he finds it convenient to do so. He is under duty to bid again only when his partner jumps the bid in a new suit or makes a cue bid.

Secondly, even if North does speak again after the three diamond bid, for example, by rebidding three hearts, South will find himself with an awkward problem on his hands. Should he go to four hearts? He then becomes assailed with certain doubts. "I wonder if partner rebid three hearts merely because he could not stand diamonds or did he continue bidding because he had a sound hand?"

Perhaps the best way to avoid both the risk and the problem is to give partner an immediate raise to three hearts. If he goes on he will find your hand a useful dummy and if he chooses to pass you should be quite convinced that you are playing the hand in the right suit. The Q 10 doubleton is surely adequate support for a reliable partner who has made a vulnerable overcall at the level of two.

Supporting partner's overcall involves different considerations. In such cases you should no longer make allowances for the possibility that partner has a four card suit. When your partner overcalls at the level of two, you may put it down in your notebook that he has a very good five card suit or a very bad habit.

And here is an intimate view of the charge taker in action.

The two suiter in contract bridge is at times an interesting phenomenon. In the hands of the skilful

player it can bring home many contracts but misman-
aged, it can lead to countless misfortunes. It has been
observed that offensively a hand containing two five
card suits should be valued at more than its actual
count. When partner is able to express a reasonable
preference these hands have greater strength than is
apparent on the surface, but in the same breath a warning must be issued to the holders of these hands in cases
where partner is unable to take a preference.

The two suiter seems to induce a certain stubborn-
ness in the possessor that he would do well to curb. I
firmly believe that the partner of the two suiter should
go out of his way to indicate a preference where one
exists. But I am also quite persuaded that where the
misfit is apparent, the player with the high cards should
retire gracefully in favor of the one with the long suit,
not only because the hand containing honor strength
will be a good dummy, but because the long suit will
be an entirely worthless affair when spread upon the
table.

On the next hand, South could have saved himself
considerable trouble had he entertained that view.

Both vulnerable. South deals.

```
                    ♠ K J 10 8 6 5 4
                    ♡ 9
                    ◇ 8 3
                    ♣ 10 4 3
   ♠ 9 7              N            ♠ A Q 2
   ♡ 8 3                           ♡ K 10 5 4 2
   ◇ Q 9 6 2     W        E        ◇ J 4
   ♣ A K 8 7 5         S           ♣ Q 9 6
                    ♠ 3
                    ♡ A Q J 7 6
                    ◇ A K 10 7 5
                    ♣ J 2
```

THE BIDDING:

South	West	North	East
1 ♡	Pass	1 ♠	Pass
2 ◇	Pass	2 ♠	Pass
3 ◇	Pass	3 ♠	Pass
4 ◇	Double	4 ♠	Double
Pass	Pass	Pass	

Opening lead: Jack of ◇

When North was unable either to show a preference for hearts or try no trump. South should have abandoned any real hopes for game. That being the case a quick checkout is in order and a pass of two spades, while it might not leave the partnership in the perfect part score position, nevertheless insures against any real disaster. Actually, the two spade contract could have been fulfilled.

But when, on the second round, South persisted to three diamonds, an action which I suppose should not be too violently condemned, and North still carried on, South should have dropped it like something ablaze. The four diamond bid was a clear invitation to the enemy to come right in with a devastating double. South had a good dummy for his partner. He couldn't expect North's hand to be very useful to himself, playing with a red suit as trump.

When the smoke had cleared away, North lost three clubs and two spades at his doubled four spade contract for a 500 point sting.

Some misfits manifest themselves through partner's failure to put in an appearance during the auction. It is all very well to be guided by standard valuation methods in bidding a hand when one contemplates the co-operation of a partner but, when partner has proven to be a washout, one should continue the fight only with cash register tricks. Take note of the rather expensive lesson that South was taught in the following hand.

Both vulnerable. South deals.

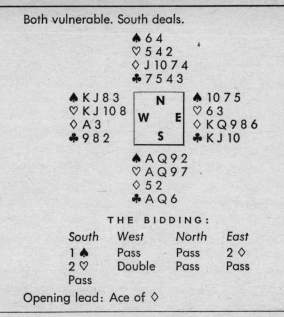

♠ 6 4
♡ 5 4 2
◊ J 10 7 4
♣ 7 5 4 3

♠ K J 8 3
♡ K J 10 8
◊ A 3
♣ 9 8 2

♠ 10 7 5
♡ 6 3
◊ K Q 9 8 6
♣ K J 10

♠ A Q 9 2
♡ A Q 9 7
◊ 5 2
♣ A Q 6

THE BIDDING:

South	West	North	East
1 ♠	Pass	Pass	2 ◊
2 ♡	Double	Pass	Pass
Pass			

Opening lead: Ace of ◊

Despite North's failure to keep the bidding open, South insisted on showing his other four card suit. West did not fall into the common error of bidding two no trump. He considered it more prudent to put the opposition to work for him. This he accomplished by the simple medium of the penalty double. The result was a three trick set for a net profit of 800 points.

North added fuel to the fire by inquiring bromidically, "Did my bidding deceive you, partner?" South attempted to justify his action on the basis of his 18 high card points.

There was no excuse for South's second bid. North, by failing to keep the opening bid alive, had confessed that his hand was trickless. At such times opener must not rely on high card points. He will be fighting single handed and must depend only on sure tricks.

Not with any reasonable stretch of optimism could South count on winning more than five or six tricks himself. This amounts to signing up for at least a 500 point contribution if doubled.

To South it is recommended that in the future he be a little more circumspect than to take on two opponents single handed. South was in effect attempting to fight tanks with a peashooter.

The correct procedure in the handling of misfits is not within the grasp of a good many players. They not only fall in love with big hands and two suiters and bid and rebid the same values several times, but even when they hold a weak hand their judgment seems to be impaired and the safest parking place is frequently missed.

In the next hand South escaped an 1100 point halocaust and actually wound up with a profit, though no credit was due him, inasmuch as his opponent made a poor choice of an opening lead.

North-South vulnerable. North deals.

```
                  ♠ 7 4 3 2
                  ♡ 2
                  ◇ A Q 4 3
                  ♣ A K 6 2
   ♠ A Q 10 9    ┌─────────┐    ♠ J
   ♡ K 7         │    N    │    ♡ A Q J 10 9
   ◇ K 9 8       │  W   E  │    ◇ 10 7 2
   ♣ Q J 10 8    │    S    │    ♣ 9 5 4 3
                 └─────────┘
                  ♠ K 8 6 5
                  ♡ 8 6 5 4 3
                  ◇ J 6 5
                  ♣ 7
```

THE ACTUAL BIDDING:

North	East	South	West
1 ◇	Pass	1 ♡	Double
Pass	Pass	Pass	

Opening lead: Queen of ♣

North opened with one diamond and South had just enough to keep the bidding open with a call of one heart. West, suspecting skulduggery, decided to take immediate action. North passed in the hope that East would respond to his partner's take-out double.

But East had his own ideas as to the best place to play the hand and passed. In this position, South might have trusted East's judgment and made an effort to run for cover. A bid of one spade, for example, offered the prospect of finding a safer landing place either in that suit or in North's original bid, diamonds. It will be seen that South can take six tricks in a spade contract.

West should have led the king of hearts. East's penalty pass must be based on a strong trump holding and it is essential to draw declarer's trumps to prevent him from getting in any ruffs. East would have overtaken the king and extracted every one of declarer's trumps. With careful defense South would probably be held to three tricks for a debit of 1,100 points.

But West, lulled into a false sense of safety by the very attractive combination of clubs, chose the queen for his lead. Declarer set out on a merry lark. Cashing two clubs, he discarded a diamond from his own hand and ruffed a club. The diamond finesse permitted him to enter dummy to ruff the last club.

Then came the ace of diamonds and a diamond ruff in the closed hand for an uninterrupted run of seven tricks. At this point South graciously conceded the remainder.

7. *Defensive Play*

BRIDGE IS ESSENTIALLY a partnership game. Nowhere is the partnership element more in evidence than in the conduct of the defense. The adventure is by no means over when the opposition has won the auction. This is the time to display the stiff upper lip, and a dedication to the task of producing the best defense may be very rewarding.

It seems that when a player is not engaged in winning a trick he cannot see the necessity for the exertion of mental effort. This is deplorable. Players should strive to let every move have a distinct meaning. They must do this to overcome the disadvantage under which they operate against declarer who has at his disposal, and in full view, all of his assets. The defenders must act as seeing eye dogs for each other and permit every card to convey some sort of message. Even in the mere following of suit you may offer your partner some clues. Meaningless plays are to be avoided. If you are interested in the suit that is being led and you desire to have it continued you should tell partner in no uncertain terms by signalling with the highest card you can spare. If you would prefer to have the suit discontinued then you play the lowest available card. In cases where you are undecided as to the best procedure you may have to shilly-shally, by that I mean play a card which is not high enough to be strongly encouraging and yet not low enough to be shouting for a discontinuance. Partner is then expected to use his own judgment as to the subsequent defense.

When, however, you have expressed your opinion in

a positive way it is not your partner's privilege "to reason why, but to do or die."

Disregarding partner's request in the defense of a hand can be excusable only if you are quite sure you can beat the hand your own way. And even then it is doubtful unless there is some feature about your hand that your partner couldn't possibly know. How many times have we heard: "I saw your signal, partner, but I couldn't see how it would do any good to lead a spade." For nonsense such as this, there is no excuse. Just because you cannot see why your partner wants a certain thing done is no excuse for failing to do so. *He* knows why. The following hand provides a splendid illustration of just that sort of thing.

Neither vulnerable. West deals.

```
                    ♠ 9 7
                    ♡ Q 6
                    ◇ J 10 7 4
                    ♣ A Q J 9 6
   ♠ A K 3            ┌─────────┐        ♠ Q 8 6 4
   ♡ 9 8 4            │    N    │        ♡ K 5 2
   ◇ K Q 8 6 5     W  │         │  E     ◇ 9 3
   ♣ 10 3            │    S    │        ♣ 8 7 5 4
                    └─────────┘
                    ♠ J 10 5 2
                    ♡ A J 10 7 3
                    ◇ A 2
                    ♣ K 2
```

THE BIDDING:

West	North	East	South
1 ◇	2 ♣	Pass	3 ♡
Pass	4 ♡	Pass	Pass
Pass			

Opening lead: King of ♠

The final contract was four hearts. West opened with one diamond and North made a very doubtful overcall of two clubs. South was unwilling to play the hand for less than game and quite properly jumped in hearts. North was undecided between three no trump and four hearts, but elected to make the latter call because of the weak spade holding. Despite holding only two hearts, he knows that partner must have at least a five card suit—and a strong one—to justify his jump bid.

The king of spades was opened and East followed with the eight. West continued with the ace and East completed his echo by playing the four. West knew that East could not be out of spades because that would give declarer six to the Q J 10, and something surely would have been heard about that suit. So West decided to shift to the king of diamonds to build up a trick in that suit. That was the end of the party. Declarer won and led a low club to the queen in dummy. The heart finesse cleared up the trumps and the king of clubs was overtaken and all losers disposed of on dummy's good suit.

West actually should have realized why East wanted a spade continuation, but even if he didn't he should have taken partner's word for it. The third spade lead forces dummy to ruff and the king of trumps cannot be picked up. When East gets in with the king of trumps he can cash a good spade before discards are taken. If declarer tries to circumvent this scheme by refusing to ruff the third spade, East wins and leads the fourth spade. This will be ruffed by West and dummy will be forced to overruff.

Partner knows best. Thousands of cases like this can be cited—where partner's strong signal should and must be obeyed. Occasionally, of course, the player on lead can safely make an intermittent play, as, for example, a king from an ace king holding, but only in such situations where he will not relinquish the lead.

Next we have a case where East could not afford to make a positive signal. It took three deuces to get the message across to his partner.

Neither vulnerable. South deals.

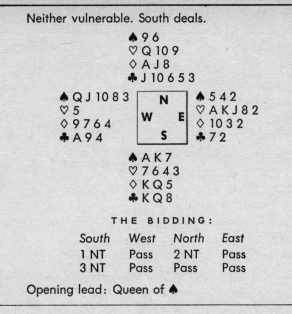

```
                    ♠ 9 6
                    ♡ Q 10 9
                    ◇ A J 8
                    ♣ J 10 6 5 3
    ♠ Q J 10 8 3    ┌─────────┐    ♠ 5 4 2
    ♡ 5             │    N    │    ♡ A K J 8 2
    ◇ 9 7 6 4       │ W     E │    ◇ 10 3 2
    ♣ A 9 4         │    S    │    ♣ 7 2
                    └─────────┘
                    ♠ A K 7
                    ♡ 7 6 4 3
                    ◇ K Q 5
                    ♣ K Q 8
```

THE BIDDING:

South	West	North	East
1 NT	Pass	2 NT	Pass
3 NT	Pass	Pass	Pass

Opening lead: Queen of ♠

Against the three no trump contract, West opened the queen of spades. East followed with the discouraging deuce and declarer won the trick with the king. In order to establish nine tricks, South must go after the clubs. He leads the king but West refuses the trick, as East follows suit with the deuce. West is in no hurry to get in, and it may be important to obtain further information from partner.

The queen of clubs is continued and also ducked. As West wins the third round of clubs, East discards the deuce of diamonds, thus completing the picture he has been trying to paint. By playing the lowest card in each of three suits, spades, clubs and diamonds, East has, by inference, suggested an interest in the fourth suit, hearts. A heart switch by West nets the defenders five more tricks.

A casual examination of the holding reveals why East couldn't get his message across in a more direct manner by signalling positively with the eight of hearts. The surrender of that card would have established declarer's seven as an eventual stopper in the suit, and the defenders would have been limited to three heart tricks and the ace of clubs.

Observe that West made two key plays on this hand, both based on the concept of partnership strategy. He did not have the cards in his own hand with which to defeat the contract, so he endeavored to obtain information from his partner. First, he held up his ace of clubs until his partner was out of the suit and could signal in another suit. Second, when West did obtain the lead, he did not routinely pursue the hopeless task of establishing his spades. West got the message and made the vital heart shift.

A bridge adage that has survived the test of generations is the one which reads: "Never signal with a queen." In other words, it is not good practice to play the queen as the top of a high-low on partner's lead of the king. It may be stated, therefore, that when an understanding partner plays the queen on partner's king it is either a singleton, or it is accompanied by the jack.

Neither vulnerable. West deals.

```
                  ♠ A Q J 6 4
                  ♡ K 9 4 3
                  ◇ 7 5
                  ♣ 10 5
  ♠ 10 8 3        ┌─────────┐      ♠ 9 5 2
  ♡ 7 5           │    N    │      ♡ 6 2
  ◇ A Q 4      W  │         │  E   ◇ J 10 9 6 2
  ♣ A K 8 6 4     │    S    │      ♣ Q J 9
                  └─────────┘
                  ♠ K 7
                  ♡ A Q J 10 8
                  ◇ K 8 3
                  ♣ 7 3 2
```

THE BIDDING:

West	North	East	South
1 ♣	1 ♠	Pass	3 ♡
Pass	4 ♡	Pass	Pass
Pass			

Opening lead: King of ♣

In this hand, South became declarer at four hearts. West opened with one club and North overcalled with one spade. East passed and South made a jump shift of three hearts, feeling that he wished to insist upon a game contract. After South's jump, North raised to game.

West opened the king of clubs and East dropped the queen. If West should continue with the ace the contract would be handed to declarer on a platter, for declarer would ruff the third round, draw the trumps and run 11 tricks. But West, reading partner for the jack of clubs, plays a low club at trick two and East is in. East has an easy shift to the jack of diamonds which yields two more tricks to the defense, and sets the contract one trick.

When it is vital to reach partner's hand in a hurry and a choice of suits is presented, many times the player is left to an out-and-out guess. The bidding will frequently provide the clue, and where such assistance is not available partner can at times act as a guide by employment of the convention known as the suit preference signal. This provides that the play of an unnecessarily high card which obviously is not a come-on signal asks partner to return the higher ranking of the remaining suits. Emphasis is placed on the phrase "which obviously is not a come-on signal," because a come-on signal is still a come-on signal and when partner leads an ace or a king and you play a high card, that means you want some more of that suit. Where the dummy makes it apparent that you couldn't possibly want that suit continued, then the convention applies. Let us see how it applied in the following hand.

North-South vulnerable. East deals.

```
                    ♠ Q 8 6
                    ♡ Q 9 2
                    ◇ K Q J 9 8 5
                    ♣ 6
  ♠ 10 7 5 3 2    ┌─────────┐    ♠ A K J
  ♡ 10 8 5        │    N    │    ♡ 6 4
  ◇ A             │ W     E │    ◇ 10 7 4
  ♣ K 9 8 2       │    S    │    ♣ Q J 10 7 4
                  └─────────┘
                    ♠ 9 4
                    ♡ A K J 7 3
                    ◇ 6 3 2
                    ♣ A 5 3
```

THE BIDDING:

East	South	West	North
1 ♣	1 ♡	2 ♣	2 ◇
Pass	2 ♡	Pass	3 ♡
Pass	4 ♡	Pass	Pass
Pass			

Opening lead: Ace of ◇

South became the declarer at a contract of four hearts and West led the ace of diamonds despite the adverse bid of that suit. It must have been apparent to every one at the table that it was a singleton ace. In following suit East played the ten of diamonds, West, mindful of his partner's opening bid of a club, then shifted to the two of that suit and school was out.

West had played very thoughtlessly. What could East have meant by the play of the ten of diamonds? It was obviously an unnecessarily high card and just as obviously could not have been intended as a come-on in diamonds. It would be absurd to assume that East had a singleton diamond since this would mean that South had six of them. The suit preference convention therefore applies, and the suggestion is being made to partner to lead the higher ranking of the remaining suits. A spade shift would have defeated the contract two tricks.

Strange to say, even without the signal from partner, West should have led a spade despite his partner's club bid. Partner is not necessarily marked with the ace of clubs, but it is a moral certainty that he has the ace of spades because without that card he would not have an opening bid. Let us suppose that he has the ace and queen of clubs, since we must assign the heart suit to South; then the only available side trick is the ace of spades.

To put it in another way—if partner does not have the ace of spades the contract cannot be defeated unless he happens to have the ace of hearts, in which case the contract will be defeated anyway. At any rate, East was quite helpful and if West couldn't use his own wits he might at least have used his partner's.

The failure to make proper use of the suit preference signal can result in disastrous swings on a single deal.

North-South vulnerable. North deals.

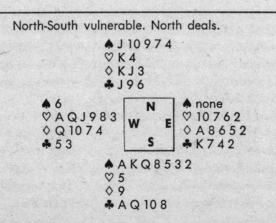

THE BIDDING:

North	East	South	West
Pass	Pass	1 ♠	2 ♡
4 ♠	Pass	6 ♠	Pass
Pass	Pass		

Opening lead: Ace of ♡

Perhaps the less said about the bidding the better. North's leap to four spades, East's failure to raise partner, and South's jump to a slam are hardly models of perfection in the art of bidding. West's non-vulnerable overcall was calculated to lay the foundation for a sacrifice bid against a probable adverse game. North had a sound raise to two spades as a free bid. If partner is unable to act, he need have no qualms about missing game. East's failure to act indicates that he has some private information on West that has not yet been divulged to us.

West led the ace of hearts and East elected to follow with the ten. That was a loud enough signal for West who, without much deliberation, continued with a heart. This permitted the discard of a diamond and when the club finesse succeeded the contract came home to roost.

I think the situation itself should have made it clear that East could hardly desire a heart continuation. Obviously, the ten was not a singleton, and obviously, too, if East, for reasons best known to himself, was anxious for a heart continuation, he could make the normal come-on signal by playing the seven.

The unusually high heart should have been taken to read:

"Partner, please lead the higher of the two remaining suits." It would not have been enough for East to leave his partner to his own devices. After all, there was no way for West to decide whether the shift should be to a club or a diamond.

Whenever mention is made of some modern development in the game, there is heard a subdued protest from a group of players who prefer to muddle through in their old fashioned way and to trust their olfactory nerve rather than the findings of the experts. They've gotten along reasonably well through the years and in their outmoded practices they find contentment.

Perhaps such players would do well to steal a page from the book of that milk vendor who proclaimed to his patrons, "My cows are not contented, they are anxious to do better."

Here is a hand on which one of the oldtimers who decries "these new fangled ideas" was unable to muddle through.

East-West vulnerable. South deals.

```
              ♠ K J 9
              ♡ 9 7 6
              ◇ A J 9 7 6
              ♣ Q 3
  ♠ A 7              N        ♠ 8 6 5 4 2
  ♡ K Q 5 3 2                 ♡ J 8
  ◇ 8 3          W       E    ◇ K 5 2
  ♣ 8 6 5 4          S        ♣ 10 9 2
              ♠ Q 10 3
              ♡ A 10 4
              ◇ Q 10 4
              ♣ A K J 7
```

THE BIDDING:

South	West	North	East
1 NT	Pass	3 NT	Pass
Pass	Pass		

Opening lead: Three of ♡

Against the contract of three no trump, West naturally led the three of hearts. The jack was permitted to hold, the eight was returned and again ducked by declarer as West won with the queen. The only heart outstanding is the ace and West could drive it out with any one of his three remaining hearts, with equal effect. Inasmuch as it made no difference to him, he did so with the deuce.

The diamond finesse lost to East whose aim it now was to put partner in to cash the setting tricks. Looking at the dummy, East cannot be blamed for returning a club and declarer scampered off with nine tricks.

When the player who has opened a suit is about to establish it finally, he may at the time he is doing so suggest to his partner his future entry by the size of the card he uses to drive out declarer's last stopper. If he does so with his lowest card, his entry is in the lower ranking of the suits in question, in this case clubs. If he establishes his suit by lead of his highest card, in this case the king, the suggested return by partner is the higher ranking suit, in this case spades.

The beauty of this convention is that it does not interfere to any great extent with any of the long established theories or conventions. It may be employed at no additional cost.

Proper discarding is another vital key to successful defense and perhaps it would be appropriate to turn our attention to this subject next.

A declarer with a long suit to run at no trump enjoys an enormous advantage over the defenders, who must fight with only half their equipment in full view. In these circumstances, it is not uncommon for eight tricks to blossom into nine.

If, however, the adversaries can perfect a method of cooperative discarding, their natural disadvantage

my be minimized. But all too often the defenders will
fall into the error of discarding from the same suit,
leaving it entirely unprotected from the enemy. This
hand from a team-of-four match provided an opportunity for sound partnership discarding.

North-South vulnerable. North deals.

```
                    ♠ 10 8
                    ♡ K 9
                    ◇ A J 8 5 3
                    ♣ K Q 7 6
   ♠ J 5 3          ┌─────────┐      ♠ K Q 9 7 6 4
   ♡ Q 7 6 4 2      │    N    │      ♡ A 10 8
   ◇ Q 9 2          │  W   E  │      ◇ K 10 7
   ♣ 10 2           │    S    │      ♣ 5
                    └─────────┘
                    ♠ A 2
                    ♡ J 5 3
                    ◇ 6 4
                    ♣ A J 9 8 4 3
```

THE BIDDING:

North	East	South	West
1 ◇	Double	Redouble	1 ♡
Pass	1 ♠	2 ♣	Pass
3 ♣	3 ♠	3 NT	Pass
Pass	Pass		

Opening lead: Three of ♠

At both tables the contract of three no trump was
reached by South and there was no variation in play
for the first four tricks. West opened the three of spades
and East's queen was permitted to hold the trick. A low
spade was returned forcing South's ace. Dummy's king
and queen of clubs were cashed: East showed out on
the second round, discarding the eight of hearts. On
the third club lead, East discarded the seven of diamonds, South played the ace, and it was now West's
turn to discard.

Instead of discarding from trick to trick as so many

players are prone to do, West realized that he must formulate a discarding campaign. After this, there were three more clubs to come, and while he himself was not in position to contribute much in the way of defensive values, he could concern himself with lightening partner's burden.

Since declarer had already shown the ace of spades and the ace of clubs, it was clear that East, for his double and subsequent bid of three spades, must have not only a string of spades headed by the king-queen, but the ace of hearts and the king of diamonds. As declarer ran the rest of clubs, it was easy to predict that East would run into a little difficulty in the selection of his discards. If he could be apprised of the fact that West holds the queen of diamonds, he would have one more safe discard to make, realizing that there was no necessity to guard the diamond king. West, therefore, signaled with the nine of diamonds on the third club lead. This effectively relieved East of any burden. He was able to bear down to the lone king of diamonds, holding on to the ace of hearts and three spades, enough tricks to defeat the contract. Declarer led a low heart to dummy's nine forcing the ace, but the defense cashed, in all, five tricks, defeating the contract.

At the other table, there was a different story to tell. West, in the manner characteristic of so many players with a bad hand, discarded indiscriminately first from one suit and then from the other, leaving partner to his own devices.

East, without anything to go on but the bidding and recalling West's discard of the deuce of diamonds, played upon the theory that declarer held the queen of diamonds. At the crucial stage, he came down to the ace of hearts, two spades and the king and another diamond, in the vain hope that declarer would try for the diamond finesse. But declarer had followed the discards carefully, and correctly reading that East had blanked

the ace of hearts, he played a low heart and ducked.
After cashing his two spades, East was hors de combat.

Now we hold no brief for East who might have shown
more enterprise by blanking the king of diamonds, but
this does not excuse West for a slipshod performance.
Even a most experienced player will appreciate a little
assistance from partner when the enemy is forcing discards.

The East hand in the next deal offers a very good
exercise in defensive discarding.

North-South vulnerable. West deals.

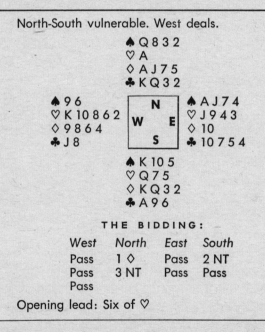

```
                      ♠ Q 8 3 2
                      ♡ A
                      ◇ A J 7 5
                      ♣ K Q 3 2
    ♠ 9 6            ┌─────────┐      ♠ A J 7 4
    ♡ K 10 8 6 2     │   N     │      ♡ J 9 4 3
    ◇ 9 8 6 4        │ W   E   │      ◇ 10
    ♣ J 8            │   S     │      ♣ 10 7 5 4
                     └─────────┘
                      ♠ K 10 5
                      ♡ Q 7 5
                      ◇ K Q 3 2
                      ♣ A 9 6
```

THE BIDDING:

West	North	East	South
Pass	1 ◇	Pass	2 NT
Pass	3 NT	Pass	Pass
Pass			

Opening lead: Six of ♡

The final contract of three no trump is natural
enough though on a good day the combined North-
South holding would produce a slam in diamonds.

West opened the six of hearts, and East played the
encouraging nine. Declarer then proceeded to run the
diamonds and East saw that he would have to arrange
to make three early discards. The first one was easy, the
three of hearts, completing his echo in that suit. Next

came the seven of spades, signaling control of that suit, and then the jack of hearts for the purpose of unblocking the suit. This, of course, was all-important. If East discards the nine of hearts instead of the jack, he will block his partner's suit when he leads it.

The important consideration is that East, looking at four clubs in dummy, must hold on to four clubs himself. Obviously West can have no more than three clubs, for the two no trump bid marks declarer with at least two. If one of West's clubs is the jack, East's four to the ten will constitute a stopper.

If declarer has both the ace and jack of clubs, hope for defeating the contract must be abandoned. If it is pointed out that dummy has four spades, and that East may be concerned with holding four cards of that suit, there is a ready answer. If South has the king of hearts, his nine tricks are in plain view—four diamonds, two hearts and three clubs. It becomes clear, therefore, that East's only vital spade is the ace.

Declarer, realizing his danger, tried to find a favorable club break and when this failed to materialize, he led a low spade from dummy with the intention of sneaking in the king. But East rose to the occasion with his ace and returned the killing heart.

It is difficult to display any personality when the opponents have reached a game or slam and you are gazing at an assortment of cards that are better adapted to the game of gin rummy than to contract bridge. Nevertheless, on those occasions it behooves one to maintain a stiff upper lip. Boredom may give away the show and enable declarer to place the missing strength in the hand of your partner.

East little suspected when he picked up his cards that he was to be the leading man of the very exciting drama upon which the curtain was about to be raised.

Both vulnerable. South deals.

```
                    ♠ 10 9 8 2
                    ♡ 6
                    ◇ A Q J 3
                    ♣ A K Q 6
  ♠ 5                    N           ♠ 7 6 4 3
  ♡ K Q J 9 8 7 5 3 2              ♡ 10
  ◇ K 4            W       E        ◇ 10 9 6 2
  ♣ 9                    S          ♣ J 7 4 2
                    ♠ A K Q J
                    ♡ A 4
                    ◇ 8 7 5
                    ♣ 10 8 5 3
```

THE BIDDING:

South	West	North	East
1 ♠	4 ♡	6 ♠	Pass
7 ♠	Pass	Pass	Pass

Opening lead: King of ♡

West's preemptive bid of four hearts prevented any scientific investigation of the hand and North's slam bid was a good gamble. South, feeling that he had rather more than he might have held, went on to a grand slam, a venture which I for one am not inclined to recommend.

The king of hearts was opened and taken by the ace. The low heart was ruffed in dummy with the ten of spades and East had to make a discard. The appearance of the dummy made a club discard out of the question, so that the temptation was to let go the deuce of diamonds. East realized, however, that holding four diamonds might be important if partner held the king (if declarer held the king there appeared to be no hope). He therefore, discarded a trump. Note that a diamond discard would have permitted South to cash four tricks in the suit after the successful finesse, and the losing club could be shed on the three of diamonds.

Declarer entered his hand with a trump and took the diamond finesse; he then drew the trumps and repeated the finesse, but when diamonds and clubs both failed to break, he had to give up a club trick at the end.

Despite East's brilliance, declarer could have made the hand. West is known to have nine hearts and one spade. The clubs and diamonds cannot, therefore, break. This is corroborated, though no corroboration is necessary, by East's discard of a trump. After ruffing the heart, declarer should return to his hand with a spade and take the diamond finesse, another trump lead permits him to repeat the diamond finesse and the king shows up out of West's hand. At this point the three top clubs should be cashed and the remaining trumps led out.

Dummy discards the six of clubs and is reduced to the ace and three of diamonds. Declarer has a diamond and a club. East who holds the ten and nine of diamonds and the jack of clubs must make a discard, which he is unable to do without committing hara-kiri.

Lead Directing Doubles

A great number of players have begun to attach an artificial significance to the penalty double insofar as it concerns the opening lead. While there are certain widely accepted lead-directing doubles, this thing can be carried too far. Such comments as "Sorry, partner, when you doubled five clubs I thought you wanted me to lead a heart" are sheer drivel. When a player doubles four spades or five clubs it is because he thinks he has the contract beaten, and not to request some peculiar lead.

There are one or two cases in which a penalty double requires certain specific leads, but this convention must not be extended beyond those limited cases. First and foremost is the double of a slam contract. The convention calls for the lead of the suit first bid by dummy. This will frequently permit third hand to obtain a ruff of the opening lead, or permit him to circumvent some psychic bid by the dummy in an effort to prevent the lead of a certain suit.

This convention would have called for a spade lead in the next hand, against which declarer would have found himself helpless.

Both vulnerable. South deals.

```
              ♠ A Q 7 2
              ♡ 10 9 8 6
              ◇ K 3
              ♣ K J 9
  ♠ 10 5           N          ♠ K J 9 8 3
  ♡ 4 3                       ♡ A
  ◇ Q J 10 9 5  W     E       ◇ 8 7 4 2
  ♣ 8 7 6 3         S         ♣ 10 5 4
              ♠ 6 4
              ♡ K Q J 7 5 2
              ◇ A 6
              ♣ A Q 2
```

THE BIDDING:

South	West	North	East
1 ♡	Pass	3 ♡	Pass
4 ◇	Double	4 ♠	Pass
5 ♣	Pass	6 ♣	Pass
6 ♡	Pass	Pass	Double
Pass	Pass	Pass	

Opening lead: Queen of ◇

The bidding was natural enough though West's double of four diamonds was an empty gesture if ever there was one. He himself would be on lead against the eventual heart contract and the only purpose it could serve was to inform the enemy of his length in diamonds.

West opened the diamond queen, an act which placed East in the throes of agonizing pain. To declarer, however, it brought little comfort, for it appeared to him that he had been granted only a momentary reprieve.

South was about to resign himself to the forlorn hope of the spade finesse when it occurred to him that the hand could be won if he were lucky enough to find East with the lone ace of hearts. On this basis he cashed the ace and king of diamonds and then the three high clubs, taking a deep breath in the process. He then played the ten of hearts. East perforce won with the ace and could return nothing which would prevent declarer from running off with his contract.

Then there are doubles of no trump contracts. If the defending side has not bid, the double of the final contract suggests but does not demand the lead of dummy's suit if no better lead is available. Where, however, the dummy's suit has been rebid, the suggestion does not apply, and the opening leader should try to find a more effective lead. Where the defending side has done some bidding, the double absolutely demands the lead of the defender's suit, and it doesn't mean maybe.

Neither vulnerable. West deals.

```
              ♠ 4 2
              ♡ A 6 2
              ◇ K J 10 9 8 4
              ♣ K 2
  ♠ K J 8 6 3   N    ♠ Q 10 5
  ♡ K Q J 3          ♡ 8 7
  ◇ A 5     W   E    ◇ 6 3 2
  ♣ 6 5         S    ♣ Q J 10 4 3
              ♠ A 9 7
              ♡ 10 9 5 4
              ◇ Q 7
              ♣ A 9 8 7
```

THE BIDDING:

West	North	East	South
1 ♠	2 ◊	Pass	2 NT
Pass	3 NT	Double	Pass
Pass	Pass		

Opening lead: King of ♡

South became declarer at a contract of three no trump after West had opened the bidding with a spade. East did not have much to be proud of except for the supporting queen of spades, but he had a feeling that the enemy had contracted for game with only one stopper in the suit. It was also clear to him that his partner's spade holding must be such that the suit would not offer an attractive opening lead. The only hope, as he saw it, was to insure the opening of his partner's suit; so he made a very sporting double. Such action is not recommended with hands this weak because of the danger of a devastating redouble, but East felt desperate.

West took no cognizance of his partner's double and selected the very fine heart sequence for his opening lead. Declarer took the first trick, drove out the ace of diamonds and was assured of nine tricks. With the spade opening four tricks would be established in that suit before the ace of diamonds was dislodged. Had partner not doubled the final contract West's lead of the king of hearts would be recommended, but under the circumstances he had no right to opinions of his own.

There is a tendency on the part of a great many players to be slipshod in the selection of the card to play in following suit. Where touching honors are held they play either one or the other indiscriminately on the theory that it "doesn't make any difference." It doesn't as far as they are concerned, but it may make a great deal of difference in the information, or rather mis-information, conveyed to partner.

False carding on the defense is rarely apt to prove profitable. In a certain number of cases declarer will be deceived, but in a great many more it is the defender's partner who will have the wool pulled over his eyes. A case where a defender deliberately false carded because he wished his partner to be deceived as to his holding in a particular suit is recorded next. East, the hero of the hand, employed a very delicate touch.

Both vulnerable. South deals.

```
                ♠ 7 5 4
                ♡ K J 10
                ◇ J 10
                ♣ A K 10 6 2
  ♠ K 8 3                        ♠ 6 2
  ♡ 9 8 6 5 3     N              ♡ A Q
  ◇ 4 3        W     E           ◇ K Q 9 8 7 6 2
  ♣ 8 4 3         S              ♣ 9 7
                ♠ A Q J 10 9
                ♡ 7 4 2
                ◇ A 5
                ♣ Q J 5
```

THE BIDDING:

South	West	North	East
1 ♠	Pass	2 ♣	2 ◇
2 ♠	Pass	4 ♠	Pass
Pass	Pass		

Opening lead: Four of ◇

The bidding was natural enough. North, having a good opening bid himself, went right to game when he learned that partner had a rebiddable spade suit and a good hand. The opening lead by West was the four of diamonds, the highest of his partner's suit. East's natural play would be the queen of diamonds, but he actually selected the king, and not because "it was all the same." On the contrary, he wished to convey to partner the impression that he did not have the queen.

If South had a solid spade suit, there was no chance to defeat the contract. But if the declarer had to lose a trump trick to West, it would be natural for West when he got the lead to continue with a diamond with the idea of overruffing dummy on the third round of the suit. East knew such play would be fruitless, since declarer could no doubt ruff high enough in his own hand to shut West out. The winning defense would be a heart shift. How could West be induced to lead a heart? Well, if he thinks declarer has the queen of diamonds he will see no other suit to attack, and East will more or less mark himself with the high hearts for his overcall. In other words, since he made a vulnerable overcall at the level of two with presumably only the king of diamonds, surely he must have some other strength outstanding in the heart suit.

When West took the king of spades he naturally shifted to a heart, and the contract was defeated a trick. A winning lie by East.

The underlead of an ace in defensive play is frequently made for deceptive purposes in order to put declarer to a guess as to the location of the outstanding honors. In many cases, however, the underlead is made because of the necessity for finding partner with the card which will give him an entry in a hurry. In the hand that follows West executed the play, but not with deceptive intent, for the bidding had made it abundantly clear that he held the ace. Nor was it made to gain immediate entry, for it was evident that dummy's king would win the trick. Actually it was for the purpose of creating a later entry into partner's hand if he happened to have the queen. Transfer of the lead to partner could be postponed for one round but after that speed was of the essence.

East-West vulnerable. North-South 30 part score, and West deals.

```
                    ♠ 5 3
                    ♡ K J
                    ♦ 10 6 3
                    ♣ A K Q 10 7 2
    ♠ K 6 2           ┌─────────┐      ♠ 7 4
    ♡ A 10 9 5 2      │    N    │      ♡ Q 7 4 3
    ♦ A K J          │ W     E │      ♦ 7 5 4 2
    ♣ 8 4            │    S    │      ♣ 9 6 3
                     └─────────┘
                    ♠ A Q J 10 9 8
                    ♡ 8 6
                    ♦ Q 9 8
                    ♣ J 5
```

THE BIDDING:

West	North	East	South
1 ♡	2 ♣	Pass	2 ♠
Pass	3 ♣	Pass	3 ♠
Pass	Pass	Pass	

Opening lead: King of ♦

The pussyfooting tempo of the bidding is accounted for by the fact that North and South held a part score of 30 points. North had a sound overcall of two clubs, and after South freely entered the auction with two spades North exercised proper restraint in bidding only three clubs instead of attempting to complete the game on that round of bidding. A four club contract might be beyond reach and South should be given the opportunity to bid three spades if he chooses. It must be presumed that he, too, is anxious to complete the game. South did bid three spades, the final contract.

West opened the king of diamonds and East played the deuce. With the solid club suit in dummy, it was necessary to get East in with reasonable promptness in order to come through the queen of diamonds declarer obviously held. While West still held the king of spades, he maintained control of the hand, so he led a low heart. Declarer had no difficulty in going up with the king, but East signalled with the seven. Declarer felt constrained to try the trump finesse and when West got in with the king of spades, he led another low heart. East's diamond return than sent declarer down to a one trick set.

Conceding one trick in order to gain three appears to be sound investment tactics. Offering a hand to illustrate the principle, might, therefore, indicate a patronizing attitude, were it not that East could well profit by the repetition.

Neither vulnerable. South deals.

```
                    ♠ 9 8
                    ♡ A 9
                    ◇ K Q 10 8 5 3
                    ♣ 6 4 3
    ♠ J 6 5 4 3 2      N       ♠ A 10
    ♡ J 7 5 2                  ♡ K 8 4 3
    ◇ 9           W       E    ◇ A 4 2
    ♣ K J              S       ♣ 10 9 7 5
                    ♠ K Q 7
                    ♡ Q 10 6
                    ◇ J 7 6
                    ♣ A Q 8 2
```

THE BIDDING:

South	West	North	East
1 ♣	Pass	1 ◇	Pass
1 NT	Pass	3 NT	Pass
Pass	Pass		

Opening lead: Four of ♠

South became declarer at the contract of three no trump. Holding 14 points, South has a mandatory opening, the minimum nature of which he designated by his rebid of one no trump. North's raise to three no trump, though aggressive, draws no objection from this corner. While the hand contains but 9 points in high cards, it is preferable to some evenly balanced hands counting to 13. The hand could well produce six tricks for the opener, two-thirds of the entire budget.

West led the four of spades and East won with the ace. He reflexly returned his partner's suit and the game was over. Declarer lost no time in clearing the diamonds, and nine tricks were there for the asking. A moment's thought should have provided East with the key to the successful defense. In all probability declarer will require the diamond suit in order to fulfill the contract. If he is deprived of the use of that long suit, the defense should have a splendid chance. East can arrange to hold up his diamond ace until the third round, hoping that the declarer will then have no more of the suit, but such tactics will avail nothing so long as dummy retains the ace of hearts for entry. If the entry card can be removed, the diamonds will not be available.

The ace of hearts must be driven out at all costs. At trick two, therefore, the proper return is the king of hearts. It is true that this play will probably cost the heart trick, but it certainly is a fair exchange for the three diamond tricks that it prevents declarer from enjoying. In bridge, very frequently penny wise is pound foolish.

No dissertation on defensive play would be complete without some reference to that cardinal sin of defenders that is reputedly a trade mark of the tyro—the presenting of declarer with a ruff and sluff. That this maneuver can be the essence of high bridge strategy, and even clearly indicated in certain situations by sound common-sense reasoning, is not nearly so well known.

We will therefore conclude this chapter with an in-

stance where the ruff and sluff, perhaps the most de-
spised play in bridge, was used three times to beat the
contract.

North-South vulnerable. West deals.

```
                    ♠ A J 9 8
                    ♡ 6
                    ◇ K Q 8 7 4
                    ♣ K J 9

    ♠ K Q 10 3        ┌─────────┐        ♠ none
    ♡ A Q 10 4 2      │    N    │        ♡ J 9 8 7 5 3
    ◇ A              │  W   E  │        ◇ 6 5 2
    ♣ 8 5 4           │    S    │        ♣ 7 6 3 2
                     └─────────┘
                    ♠ 7 6 5 4 2
                    ♡ K
                    ◇ J 10 9 3
                    ♣ A Q 10
```

THE BIDDING:

West	North	East	South
1 ♡	Double	4 ♡	4 ♠
Double	Redouble	Pass	Pass
Pass			

Opening lead: Ace of ♡

North doubled West's opening bid of one heart and
East justifiably jumped to four. Barricading tactics
might result in South selecting an inferior contract.

South actually chose to bid four spades and West,
seeing an easy way out of the current tax problem,
doubled. North, thinking along the same lines, redoubled, and East's standing for the redouble is a mas-
terpiece of brazenness. But then perhaps it is not fitting
for me to labor the point in view of the outcome of this
episode.

West opened the ace of hearts and dropped declarer's
king. West observed that a heart continuation might
play havoc with declarer's trumps, so he continued the
suit. South, of course, could not afford to ruff in

dummy without setting up a second trump trick for West. Winning in his own hand South led a trump and permitted West's queen to hold the trick. West continued with a third round of hearts and again declarer ruffed in the closed hand, leaving himself with two trumps. He led one of them and finessed the jack in dummy. Declarer could return to his hand and make the final finesse to pick up all the trumps but he could not prevent West from getting in with the ace of diamonds and cashing the rest of the hearts. So he postponed the drawing of trumps to lead the king of diamonds. West won and led a fourth round of hearts. This forced South's last trump and made it impossible to pick up West's trumps.

8. *Who's Wrong?*

IN MY TRIPS around the country, naturally enough, I am frequently asked to act as umpire on hands where something went wrong, many saved for months. Fortunately, by the time these discussions are thrust upon me, most of the heat is off, and everyone truly desires enlightenment, instead of merely wishing to prove that his partner was either a fool or a knave. Also fortunately, in most cases it is not necessary to place the entire burden of guilt on either partner. They've usually been the victims of their own mutual Dis-Aid Society.

Let's sit in as jury on a few hands.

North, South vulnerable. South deals.

```
              ♠ 10 6 2
              ♡ Q 10 5 2
              ◇ A 8
              ♣ A Q 6 3
♠ A K Q J 8 7   ┌───────┐   ♠ 9 5 4 3
♡ J 8 4         │   N   │   ♡ 7
◇ 9           W │       │ E ◇ K Q 6 2
♣ K 7 5         │   S   │   ♣ J 10 4 2
              └───────┘
              ♠ void
              ♡ A K 9 6 3
              ◇ J 10 7 5 4 3
              ♣ 9 8
```

THE BIDDING:

South	West	North	East
Pass	4 ♠	Pass	Pass
Pass			

Opening lead: Two of ♡

After a pass by South, West elected to gamble it out with a bid of four spades, which was passed all around. The two of hearts was opened and South won with the king. He then shifted to the nine of clubs. Declarer played low and North won with the queen, cashed the ace on which South dropped the eight and North continued with the third club. Since South could not ruff, West won the trick, drew trumps and discarded his losing diamond on dummy's jack of clubs. You can see that this performance would give rise to some discussion, particularly when it can be seen that North and South could easily have made five hearts.

North claims South should have opened the bidding, South contends that North should have doubled the four spade bid, whereupon South would have overridden the double with a call of five hearts. South charges that North should have cashed the setting trick with the ace of diamonds. North argues that South should not have led high low in clubs as if he wanted to ruff the third round. It's all very involved.

Despite the fact that the hand lacks the textbook requirements, I have no objection to an occasional opening bid with the South hand. It has great playing power if partner happens to have a preference, and in order to find out if one exists, an early start must be made; otherwise the bidding might readily get out of hand before both suits can be shown. If South does elect to open, a heart bid should be preferred. A later bid of five diamonds, will not be surrounded with as much danger in that sequence.

North might hazard a double of four spades, but I do not believe his pass is subject to the slightest criticism. And if he did double, it is by no means certain that South would have selected hearts. He might have chosen his six card suit, which in this case would not have worked.

I agree that South's better return would be the eight of clubs instead of the nine, but North should still have saved the day by cashing the ace of diamonds. The four spade bid surely was based on a six card suit and South would, therefore, have no trumps. That is a moral certainty, whereas the fear that West had no diamonds was rather far fetched.

In the next case the blame is easy to place. The villain in question was South, who is known to the trade as a "charge taker." We present herein a grim portrayal of this particular villain in action.

Both vulnerable. South deals.

```
              ♠ J 9 5 2
              ♡ 8
              ◊ Q J 10 6 5
              ♣ 9 8 5
 ♠ 4 3                        ♠ Q 10 8 7 6
 ♡ 6            N             ♡ J 10 9 7 4
 ◊ A K 9 8 7 3  W   E         ◊ 2
 ♣ Q J 4 2         S          ♣ 10 6
              ♠ A K
              ♡ A K Q 5 3 2
              ◊ 4
              ♣ A K 7 3
```

THE BIDDING:

South	West	North	East
2 ♡	3 ◊	Double	Pass
3 ♡	Pass	3 NT	Pass
4 ♣	Pass	4 ♡	Pass
6 ♡	Pass	Pass	Double
Pass	Pass	Pass	

Opening lead: King of ◊

South's opening two heart bid will pass muster in any league. Not much will be required from partner to produce a slam. West's bid of three diamonds is pointless in the extreme. In view of South's announcement of great strength, the bid amounts to barking at the moon.

North's double was from the heart and should have resulted in a harvest of 1,400 points. South's refusal to stand for the double shows the instincts of the "charge-taker" at his very height. He argued that he did not wish to miss a slam if there was one.

This is unsound reasoning. I think it is sound reasoning for him to assume that his partner likes slams just as much as he does, and if he thought there was any chance for slam he would not double the three diamond bid. South had a perfect hand for defense against diamonds and should have been delighted to leave it in.

When North did the next best thing and went to three no trump, South had overstayed the mark and should have rested there. When he bid four clubs, North was more or less obliged to return to hearts. South's leap now to six hearts was not far removed from madness. He was defeated 1,100 points, for a net swing of 2,500 points.

While the trump break was unfortunate, it should not have been remote from contemplation. South might have taken soundings. From the circumstances that West, though vulnerable, was willing to undertake a nine trick contract against a demand bid, it may be assumed that he is short in hearts, and if North cannot support the suit, which his double and subsequent three no trump bid suggest, they can be expected to be stacked in the East hand.

Where a partner has painted a reasonably accurate picture of his holdings, it seems to be the better part of valor to abide by his decision.

The road hog that we sometimes encounter on the highway is a much less sinister individual than his counterpart one so frequently engages at the bridge table.

Not sufficient emphasis has ever been placed upon the partnership factor in bidding. There is too much assumption of responsibility by one player in the making of decisions in doubtful cases, when discretion would call for a consultation with partner. Such a consultation is available by means of the forcing pass, which permits partner to decide.

East, West vulnerable. South deals.

```
              ♠ 2
              ♡ 10 9 4
              ◇ Q J 9 5
              ♣ A Q 7 5 3
♠ 9 8 6 5        N        ♠ Q J 10 3
♡ Q 6 2      W     E      ♡ K 8 7
◇ 4              S        ◇ A K 7 6 3
♣ J 10 9 4 2             ♣ 8
              ♠ A K 7 4
              ♡ A J 5 3
              ◇ 10 8 2
              ♣ K 6
```

THE ACTUAL BIDDING:

South	West	North	East
1 ♠	Pass	2 ♣	2 ◇
2 ♡	Pass	2 NT	Pass
3 NT	Pass	Pass	Pass

South opened with one spade and partner responded with two clubs. East, though vulnerable, came in with two diamonds and South made what appears to be the very normal rebid of two hearts. North, in view of partner's free rebid, went on to two no trump and South carried on to game. Against the proper opening of the queen of spades, declarer could take no more than eight tricks.

It is South's rebid that is the subject of our observation. North contended that his partner should have passed the two diamond bid around to him. This bid he would have doubled for a set of 800 points. South maintained that there was no way for him to know that his partner could double two diamonds. To which North replied, "You could pass and find out."

"But what if you were unable to do anything over the two diamond bid?" was South's query. North properly contended, "You might have trusted me. With sound values I would hardly permit the opposition to steal the hand from a partner who has opened the bidding."

I am inclined to sympathize with North's view. In fact, several experts to whom this hand was submitted went so far as to double the two diamond bid themselves with the South hand on the theory that if North had an unbalanced hand he would not stand for the double, and if he had a more or less normal hand that justified entering the two level, the penalty would be adequate.

While this view may be somewhat extreme, nevertheless it shows a tendency on the part of experienced players to look for vulnerable sets on hands where it is not clearly indicated that a game can be scored.

Various bids at contract have had their enthusiastic proponents. But the most subtle, and perhaps the most interesting of calls, has been peculiarly neglected. I refer, of course, to the pass. Most players can be taught the management of various artificial conventions; many acquire the ability to execute coups and end plays, but few ever learn the gentle strategy of silence.

The pass has come to denote a confession of weakness. But it need not be so. The pass has many versions. It may be the act of one who lies in ambush, waiting for the enemy to make a false step. It may be the act of a player who is conferring upon partner the courtesy of letting him make the final decision. In some cases it may actually be the strongest call in contract, namely the forcing pass. To illustrate, visualize the situation in which you have bid six spades. Your right hand opponent has made a sacrifice bid of seven clubs. A pass by you is the strongest type of action inasmuch as it indicates a willingness to have partner contract for a grand slam. If you are not interested in a grand slam, you would double the opponents yourself.

East, West vulnerable. South deals.

```
              ♠ K J 10 5
              ♡ A J 5 4
              ◇ 10 9
              ♣ K 9 3
  ♠ none          N        ♠ A Q 8 6 4 3 2
  ♡ 8 6 3 2    W     E     ♡ 7
  ◇ 7 6 5 3 2     S        ◇ K J 4
  ♣ Q J 6 4               ♣ 8 5
              ♠ 9 7
              ♡ K Q 10 9
              ◇ A Q 8
              ♣ A 10 7 2
```

THE ACTUAL BIDDING:

South	West	North	East
1 ♡	Pass	3 ♡	3 ♠
4 ♡	Pass	Pass	Pass

In this hand South missed the bus. He played the hand at a game in hearts, handled the dummy very well, and succeeded in making five odd, which pleased him no end. Speaking in terms of lost opportunities, he had tossed away the tidy sum of 650 points, for a 1,100 point set was there for the asking. Should South have doubled the three spade bid? I think not. But South had nothing to lose and everything to gain by passing the bid of three spades. When responder has made a jump bid, both partners are unconditionally obligated to go to game, or collect the equivalent in tariff.

South's pass would not have been a confession of weakness. It would merely announce: "Partner, I am giving you the courtesy of the road. You may wish to bid three no trump, or you may think it profitable to double the enemy. If neither of these ideas appeals to you, it will be incumbent upon you to bid four hearts."

When the three spade bid got around to North, he would not have had a difficult decision on his hand. A penalty of more than the value of game was clearly in sight and the double would have been routine. Silence, once again, would have proven to be golden.

The forcing pass may be made for quite another reason, and in this hand from an important tournament some interesting variations occurred.

East and West vulnerable. South deals.

```
                    ♠ K 4
                    ♡ 4 3 2
                    ◇ 7 5 3
                    ♣ Q J 8 6 4
   ♠ 9 8 6                        ♠ A Q J 10 7 3 2
   ♡ 8 7          N               ♡ 10 9
   ◇ J 9 2     W     E            ◇ K 10 8 4
   ♣ 10 9 7 5 3     S             ♣ none
                    ♠ 5
                    ♡ A K Q J 6 5
                    ◇ A Q 6
                    ♣ A K 2
```

THE BIDDING:

South	West	North	East
2 ♡	Pass	2 NT	3 ♠
Pass	Pass	3 NT	Pass
4 NT	Pass	6 NT	Pass
Pass	Pass		

The opening bid of two hearts was uniformly made and I believe most players responded with two no trump. Where East overcalled with three spades, what would you do as South? Instinctively, a vast majority of players would bid four hearts. Actually, that is not the proper procedure. The fact that South is not absolutely sure of making the contract is only a minor objection. The real reason is that it is not necessary for South to decide what to do. The opening two bid has obligated both partners to continue until game is reached or the enemy penalized. If North happens to have a spade stopper no trump might be a safer contract than hearts. Furthermore, the opposition is vulnerable and North might have a sound double of the three spade contract. Everything is to be gained and nothing is to be lost by the pass.

When North announced the spade stopper (in this sequence of bids his second no trump bid indicates protection in the adverse suit), South decided he was reasonably safe for ten tricks and invited the slam. On the basis of his club holding, North accepted the invitation.

East elected to make the neutral opening of a heart and declarer in running down six tricks in that suit placed the enemy in such a squeeze position that he took all thirteen tricks.

In some cases a contract of six hearts was reached after North had shown the clubs. This permitted East to double the slam and the lead of dummy's suit immediately defeated the contract.

Players holding a distribution of 4–3–3–3 are frequently heard to remark: "Partner, I had such splendid distribution for no trump that I thought I would stretch a point to give you a raise without the prescribed high card values."

Let us examine the question calmly. The truth of the matter is that hands of that distribution are so seriously handicapped that, if game is to be achieved, resort must usually be had to the shortest road, one that is only nine tricks long. Curiously enough, the best no trump distribution is not 4–3–3–3. Our own choice would be for a solid six card suit (or longer), and three aces on the side. Yet there are a great many players who simply will not permit partner to play a hand at no trump if they themselves hold a six card suit. Witness this hand.

North and South vulnerable. West deals.

```
              ♠ 8 4
              ♡ A K 10 9 5 2
              ◇ K 10 3
              ♣ 10 9
♠ A 10 9 6 2    ┌─────┐    ♠ Q J 3
♡ 4             │  N  │    ♡ 8 7 6
◇ A Q J 5       │W   E│    ◇ 8 7 6
♣ K 8 7         │  S  │    ♣ 5 4 3 2
                └─────┘
              ♠ K 7 5
              ♡ Q J 3
              ◇ 9 4 2
              ♣ A Q J 6
```

THE BIDDING:

West	North	East	South
1 ♠	2 ♡	Pass	2 NT
Pass	3 ♡	Pass	Pass
Pass			

Opening lead: Queen of ♠

West opened with one spade and North overcalled with two hearts. South, buoyed up by partner's overcall, naturally had visions of game and tried two no trump. There are many players who would have gone all the way to three with his hand, but the lack of a diamond stopper was a natural deterrent to such action.

North's rebid of three hearts is in our opinion not good tactics. He has the type of hand that will develop well at no trump and he should chance a raise to game. His two worthless doubletons are no help at all in playing at hearts, but can conceivably be useful if partner has three or four of each suit with as little as a queen-jack holding. South realized that his hand could not be expected to produce sufficient tricks at hearts because of his barren distribution, and since partner did not appear to like no trump, he checked out of the auction.

By fine cooperative defense the part score contract was actually defeated. The queen of spades was opened and not covered, West playing the encouraging six. The jack of spades was continued and again not covered. At this point West made a very thoughtful discard. He did not complete the echo but played the nine of spades, suggesting to partner that he did not wish any more leads in that suit. It was important to establish diamond tricks before the king of clubs was lost. East obediently shifted to the eight of diamonds. West won the ace and returned the queen.

Declarer subsequently took the club finesse and when it failed went down one on his bid. He could have fulfilled the contract by not attempting the club finesse. Running out all his trumps, he could have placed West in an impossible position at the end where a diamond throw-in would have compelled West to lead into dummy's ace-queen of clubs. But this same end play would have been available to South at no trump and would have permitted the scoring of a game. West would presumably open the ten of spades. By the time declarer ran his six heart tricks West would have found it impossible to hold onto all four spades and the diamond and club stoppers.

One should beware of the 4–3–3–3. It's a wolf in sheep's clothing. Here is another case in point.

Both vulnerable. South deals.

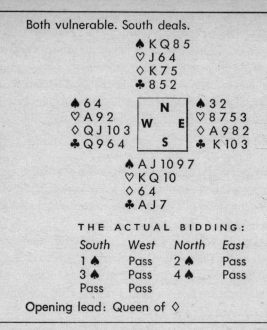

♠ K Q 8 5
♥ J 6 4
♦ K 7 5
♣ 8 5 2

♠ 6 4   ♠ 3 2
♥ A 9 2   ♥ 8 7 5 3
♦ Q J 10 3   ♦ A 9 8 2
♣ Q 9 6 4   ♣ K 10 3

♠ A J 10 9 7
♥ K Q 10
♦ 6 4
♣ A J 7

THE ACTUAL BIDDING:

South	West	North	East
1 ♠	Pass	2 ♠	Pass
3 ♠	Pass	4 ♠	Pass
Pass	Pass		

Opening lead: Queen of ♦

The bidding is strictly routine up to North's final bid which in my opinion was not sound. North should have passed his partner's three spade bid without any genuine fear of missing a game. He argued that he held considerably more than he might have had for his mild raise to two spades and, therefore, felt justified in accepting his partner's invitation to go game. As will be seen, declarer had no reasonable play for the contract.

I cannot quite agree with North's estimate of his hand. Looks were deceiving. A prospective dummy should be judged by the number of actual tricks it will probably develop for partner. Viewed from that standpoint, the hand is poor indeed. At the most liberal estimate, this holding will produce only three tricks for partner, which will require his taking seven tricks himself. This is too much to ask for. If South held that many winners, he would have hopped right to four spades after the raise. When the bidding proceeds in this manner, North should have a likelihood of taking four tricks before accepting partner's invitation to go game. In valuing hands in support of partner, a definite deduction should be made when responder holds a 4–3–3–3 distribution. Another problem here is that the four trump holding, desirable as it seems, becomes less useful when there are no short suits to use them on. That's why a point should be deducted with this type of distribution.

To put it in another way, North values his hand originally at nine points in support of spades, which would render it a very sound raise, but when the one point deduction is made for the balanced hand, it becomes worth only eight points and is reduced to a courtesy type raise. When the opening bidder extends an invitation to go on to game, the responder should respectfully decline if he holds a mere courtesy raise.

When a slam contract is under consideration, the opening bidder should make certain that his partner is really interested in going beyond game, before he extends an invitation.

In the next hand, South managed to bring home the apparently impossible contract that an overenthusiastic partner had thrust upon him.

North-South vulnerable. South deals.

```
                    ♠ A K Q J
                    ♡ K 5 3
                    ◇ A K 2
                    ♣ A 7 2
        ♠ 6              N          ♠ 8 7 5
        ♡ J 9                       ♡ Q 10 6 4 2
        ◇ J 10 9 8 3   W    E       ◇ Q 7 5
        ♣ K J 9 8 6        S        ♣ Q 10
                    ♠ 10 9 4 3 2
                    ♡ A 8 7
                    ◇ 6 4
                    ♣ 5 4 3
```

THE BIDDING:

South	West	North	East
Pass	Pass	2 NT	Pass
3 ♠	Pass	5 ♠	Pass
Pass	Pass		

Opening lead: Jack of ◊

North, holding 24 points and a balanced hand, properly opened with two no trump and South, with four high card points and a five card suit, made the normal response of three spades. He was willing to pass a three no trump rebid but with only one high card he felt the hand might be more manageable in a suit contract.

North, under the impression that a slam was in the offing, jumped to five spades as an invitation for his partner to proceed with a suitable holding.

This was highly improper, for South's response did not promise any special values and he might readily have had a long spade suit with no high card strength.

If North wished to suggest a slam, he should have done so below the game level by cue bidding in clubs or diamonds. It would then be up to South to make any further try.

West opened the jack of diamonds and declarer was faced with the loss of two clubs and a heart. The outlook was dismal, but not altogether hopeless. In order to bring in the contract, he would have to find a very favorable defensive holding in hearts and clubs.

He drew trumps and stripped both hands of diamonds. He then gave up a club trick without cashing the ace. Declarer won the return with the ace of clubs and cashed the A-K of hearts.

At this point, due to the fortunate break in distribution, declarer had the hand made regardless of whether he led a club or a heart. If he led a heart, East would win and, having nothing but hearts would have to give declarer a ruff in one hand and the discard of a club in the other.

If declarer chose to get out with a club, West would win, and must commit suicide by leading a diamond or a club.

The informatory double as a means of showing strength when an opponent has opened the bidding has come to be reasonably well understood by the public. But that this same bid is available as a weapon also to the person who has opened the bidding himself but has not yet heard from partner, does not seem to register with many players.

Both sides vulnerable. South deals.

```
                ♠ 8 6 2
                ♡ K 10 5 3
                ◇ 10 7 3
                ♣ 6 4 2
  ♠ K Q J 9 7   ┌─────────┐   ♠ A 10 5 3
  ♡ Q 4         │    N    │   ♡ J 7 2
  ◇ J 9 8       │ W     E │   ◇ 6 4
  ♣ A 8 7       │    S    │   ♣ 10 9 5 3
                └─────────┘
                ♠ 4
                ♡ A 9 8 6
                ◇ A K Q 5 2
                ♣ K Q J
```

THE SUGGESTED BIDDING:

South	West	North	East
1 ◇	1 ♠	Pass	Pass
Double	Pass	2 ♡	Pass
4 ♡	Pass	Pass	Pass

South opens the bidding with one diamond, which is properly overcalled by West with one spade. North and East pass in due course, especially North. South, of course, is in no mood to give up and naturally must take some action, despite his partner's far away look.

It would be highly improper for South merely to rebid two diamonds, and it would be equally unsound to contest with a simple bid of two hearts. The proper procedure to show a powerful opening bid and a flexible hand is to double. This, of course, is still a takeout double, because partner has not yet bid. The double, however, gives partner a number of choices. He may bid hearts, he may bid clubs, he may return to diamonds, he may bid no trump, or in some cases might leave the double in for penalties if such action should appear to be profitable.

When I saw this hand played the South player doubled the bid of one spade and North responded with two hearts. This is the proper call rather than a return to partner's bid suit. When partner has made a takeout double we should go to great lengths to show any major suit holding. South then raised to three hearts and North decided to pass. An easy game was missed.

Upon whose shoulders should rest the blame for missing the boat? Concededly this is a close case. South argued that if his partner had nothing, the losses added up to a spade, a club, and two hearts; that if he were sure his partner had the king of hearts he would have contracted for game himself. I had to allow certain merit to his argument, but all things considered I think he might have gambled it out himself. North might have only the queen of hearts and with a little luck the trump losers could be held to one trick, or North might have five little hearts in which case the game will be easy if the suit happens to break. This is the type of hand on which South might take the strain off his partner. If all you need from partner is a king or a queen to produce game, you ought to take a chance that he has that much.

Recent years have brought many changes in the character of bridge players. The timid souls of yesterday have been converted into the tyrants of today. They impose their tyranny with a weapon against which partner can be rendered completely helpless. Those mild mannered souls who in the earlier days rarely ventured above the game level take great delight in rousing partner from the serenity of a game contract by uttering the four no trump call, converting partner into a galley slave. That the number of aces held may not be altogether material does not even remotely concern the asking type player. Observe this case.

Both vulnerable. North deals.

```
                  ♠ K 9 3
                  ♡ A K Q 9 6 4
                  ◇ K J 7
                  ♣ 7
    ♠ J 10 2        N           ♠ Q 5
    ♡ 8 7 5                     ♡ 10 3 2
    ◇ 4 2        W      E       ◇ 9 8 5
    ♣ A J 9 6 5     S           ♣ Q 10 4 3 2
                  ♠ A 8 7 6 4
                  ♡ J
                  ◇ A Q 10 6 3
                  ♣ K 8
```

THE ACTUAL BIDDING:

North	East	South	West
1 ♡	Pass	1 ♠	Pass
3 ♡	Pass	4 ◇	Pass
4 ♠	Pass	4 NT	Pass
5 ◇	Pass	5 ♠	Pass
Pass	Pass		

Opening lead: Ace of ♣

The opening bid of one heart, the response of one spade, and the rebid of three hearts fall into natural molds. The next two bids are also routine. South, counting the combined assets, properly reached the conclusion that there were enough available for slam purposes. Whereupon he took matters into his own hand

and subjected partner to the inquisition with a bid of four no trump. North dutifully responded, showing one ace, and South became seized with qualms. Since the ace of clubs was missing, he now became concerned about a possible spade loser and called things off with a bid of five spades. This gave North no further choice in the matter. He was obliged to check out, and the contract was fulfilled to the trick. Gratification at having stopped "on a dime" blinded the North and South players to the fact that slam could have been made in hearts, diamonds and no trump.

If South had not taken over complete authority but had permitted the partnership the use of dual control, the partners might have had an opportunity to consult as to the best contract. After North's return to four spades, South might have made a descriptive bid of five diamonds, showing two five card suits. North would then raise to six diamonds, anticipating that any losing spades would be discarded on North's good hearts, and also giving his partner the choice of suits.

At one table when South, also using Blackwood, signed off at five spades, North took the law into his own hand and bid six spades. This is a violation of the Blackwood convention and was justly punished. However, if North was bound to disregard the rules of the Blackwood convention, he might as well have tried six diamonds, rather than six spades. He had already supported spades, and partner would in this manner be offered a choice. Having more solid diamonds, he would have chosen that suit as trump, with a happy ending.

APPENDICES

Duplicate Bridge Strategy

THE POINTS OF VARIANCE between duplicate contract and rubber bridge are fewer than is commonly supposed. In rubber bridge it is the big hands (or those involving big penalties) that really matter. In duplicate bridge with match-point scoring, every hand counts. In fact, every hand counts exactly as much as every other hand, and one producing a contract of 2 clubs weighs just as heavily in the scales as one that produces 7 no trump.

Each deal in a match-point duplicate game is a separate contest. The purpose of each pair is to do better than the other pairs. *How much* better is not really important, as examination of the following "travelling score slip" (that is, the record of all the times a certain deal was played) will indicate:

BOARD 4

N-S vs. Pair No.	E-W Pair No.	Contract	N-S +	N-S −	N-S Match-Points
1	1	4 ♠	620		3
2	3	3 NT	600		1½
3	5	3 NT	600		1½
4	2	3 NT	630		4
5	4	5 ♡ x	1400		5
6	6	5 ♠		100	0

Match-point scoring is accomplished in this manner: The scores of the pairs which played the same cards are compared. Each pair receives 1 match-point for each other pair with a lower score, and ½ match-point for each other pair with the same score.

Observe the results of the North-South pairs on the deal (designated as Board 4) which is scored above. Pair 5 was able to double an opposing 5 heart contract and to defeat it 1,400 points. This score beat the results obtained by the other five North-South pairs, whereupon Pair 5 gets 1 match-point from each of them, a total of 5 match-points. Pair 4 had the next-best North-South score; it beat four other pairs and receives 4 match-points. Pair 1 beat three other pairs and receives 3 match-points.

The +1,400 score of Pair 5 was 770 points better than the score of Pair 4, yet Pair 5 receives only 1 match-point more than Pair 4. And Pair 4 has the same 1-point advantage over Pair 1, whose score it beat by only 10 points.

Opening Bids

My tactics in the matter of opening bids at match-point duplicate do not vary widely from those employed in rubber bridge. A slight relaxation of the requirements has been found profitable when the prospective opener holds a suit headed by the Ace and King. The advantage is to be found in the assurance that the best opening lead will be obtained should the final contract fall to the adversaries.

The importance of the opening lead can hardly be overestimated at match-point play.

And in third position, whether vulnerable or not, I never pass holding a biddable suit headed by the two top honors.

It Doesn't Pay to "Shoot"

Although the objective in match-point duplicate is to beat the other pairs, this does not mean that you should make a direct effort to make a big score on every hand. Such tactics may yield a few "tops," when you have the best score on the board, but gambling bidding will inevitably lead to an even greater number of "bottoms," when you have the worst score. A "top-or-bottom" style of bidding is losing play in duplicate bridge.

For example, you are South and hold this hand:

♠ A J x   ♡ A Q 10 x x   ◇ J 10 x x   ♣ J

The bidding has proceeded:

South	West	North	East
1 ♡	Pass	1 NT	Pass
2 ♡	Pass	2 NT	Pass
?			

At rubber bridge, you might decide to push on to 3 no trump. You realize that this is a gambling bid, but the gamble is worth while. Making a game is worth 500 to 600 points; making a part score is worth no more than 150 points. For the chance for increased profit you can risk going down a trick, or perhaps going down an additional trick.

But in duplicate this gamble is not a good one. If you stop at 2 no trump, the mere fact that you are in a no trump contract, in which the first trick counts 40 points, will give you a better score than pairs which stop at a heart or other suit contract and take the same number of tricks that you do. If you gamble on 3 no trump and go down, these pairs will automatically beat you. The fact that a successful game contract might add several hundred points to your total-point score does not influence you; in match-point scoring you are not interested in the extent of your advantage over other pairs. Any advantage at all is sufficient.

This point was first forcibly brought home to me in an important Canadian-American championship. On the hand which comes to mind the bidding had progressed to 2 no trump, at which point it was clearly indicated that I should pass. However, it was near the end of the session, and feeling, as I did, that drastic measures were in order, I stretched to 3 no trump, which, due to an error in the defense, I was permitted to make for a score of plus 600. There were 24 tables in play and when the scores were posted, I observed that I had attained a complete top score of 23 points. I also noted, however, that had I been content to pass at 2 no trump a score of plus 150 would have yielded 22 points. It occurred to me, therefore, what a "sucker" I had actually been. I had risked perhaps 20 points in order to gain an additional 1.

On the same reasoning, you should not bid doubtful slams in a duplicate game. When a slam is at all close, at least half of the other pairs, and possibly two-thirds of them, will fail to reach it. If you gamble on a slam, you risk losing to all these pairs in order to tie the minority who will bid the slam.

In an effort to obtain the maximum score, many players will strain to play a slam at no trump instead of a major suit, or to play in a doubtful major instead of a minor suit. If the higher-ranking contract is just as safe as the lower, naturally it should be selected. It has been my observation, however, that in the long run it will prove more profitable to select for the final slam contract that suit which offers the greatest safety. In this respect, the leaning should be more in the direction of rubber bridge tactics. The reason is that a vast majority of slam contracts, though they are not played in the maximum contract, will yield an above-average

score. The risk entailed in seeking a higher-ranking
contract is frequently not commensurate with the increase in the number of match points that the higher
contract yields.

Watching the Vulnerability

For making a vulnerable game in duplicate, you
add 500 points to your score. Since the trick-score must
be at least 100 points, a vulnerable game contract bid
and made must total at least 600.

When you have a choice between doubling the opponents and making a game of your own, vulnerability
decides the issue far more often than it does in rubber
bridge. Suppose you are vulnerable and your opponents are not, and you hold:

♠ J x   ♡ A J x   ◇ K 10 x x   ♣ K J x x

Your partner is the dealer and bids 1 spade. Next hand
overcalls with 2 diamonds. In rubber bridge, you would
double. In duplicate, if you were not vulnerable, or if
your opponents were vulnerable, you would double.
The 2 diamond overcaller is getting a very bad trump
break, and should go down three tricks even if he had a
sound overcall.

Inasmuch as you are vulnerable against non-vulnerable opponents, there is some doubt as to the wisdom of
doubling. There is a strong likelihood that you can
make game, for a score of 600 or more. Now, should it
develop that you can punish the adverse contract to
the extent of only three tricks, for 500 points, your action will prove disastrous. However, if a four-trick
sting can be inflicted, the 700 points should yield a top
score or close to it. The conservative procedure is to go
for game, the aggressive step is to try for the four-trick
penalty.

In rubber bridge, no such anxious moment is presented. A sure profit of at least 500 points is there to be taken. And the double is the proper procedure in order to "sweeten the kitty." After this hand the odds will still remain 3 to 1 in favor of your winning the rubber.

While taking sure profits in rubber bridge is sound business it is not necessarily so in duplicate because all profits are comparative.

In rubber bridge, you make a preëmptive bid when you are sure you cannot go down more than 500 points. In duplicate, you cannot do this against non-vulnerable opponents. Making a non-vulnerable game adds a bonus of only 300 points to the trick-score, so that the maximum score for bidding a game (and making less than a slam) is 460. You cannot risk a loss of 500 points to keep your opponents from making a score of 400 to 460 points.

As a matter of fact, preëmptive bids in general are not so sound in duplicate as they are in rubber bridge. When the strength is evenly divided between the two sides, making a part score of 2 spades may be the best either side can do. If you make a preëmptive 3 spade bid and go down one, you will have a very bad score.

Free Raises

Free raises when partner's opening bid has been overcalled should still be sound, though somewhat more shading is permitted in duplicate bridge. However, the shading must not be carried too far.

For example: As South, with the opponents vulnerable, you hold:

♠ Q 10 x x x x
♡ x
◊ 10 x
♣ J x x

The bidding has progressed:

North	East	South
1 ♠	2 ♡	?

A raise to 2 Spades is not recommended. Better procedure is to pass and await developments. If the opponents should reach a 4 heart contract, you will naturally wish to sacrifice at 4 spades, but if you make an immediate free raise, you may find yourself in a position where you are called upon to make a very difficult decision later on in the auction. If you pass first and compete violently in spades thereafter, partner knows that you have trumps and distribution but no honor strength.

Choice of Contracts

The fact that spades and hearts count 30 per trick, as against 20 per trick for diamonds and clubs, often makes it wise to choose a higher-scoring contract in preference to a safer one. Suppose you hold:

♠ J x x   ♡ Q 10 x x   ◇ K x x x   ♣ x x

Partner opens with 1 diamond. In rubber bridge you might respond by raising to 2 diamonds. It is a safe contract, and unless partner can rebid over 2 diamonds there is no possible hope of game. At duplicate, your response would be 1 heart; you cannot surrender the opportunity of getting into a major suit.

Now partner rebids 1 spade. At rubber bridge you would return to the safer 2 diamond contract; partner probably has only a four-card spade suit and may have a five-card diamond suit, and even if he has only four diamonds, your added length in that suit would make it safer. But at duplicate, you pass 1 spade. If by chance you can make the same number of tricks in spades and diamonds, the 2 spade contract will be far better. If you can make one more trick at diamonds, a 2 spade contract fulfilled will still be as good as a 3 diamond contract.

Overcalls

In Duplicate Bridge a slight modification is advised in the direction of the freer use of overcalls. At rubber bridge, one bad bid might cause you the afternoon's profits. At duplicate, an error in judgment will result at most in the loss of that particular hand.

Any reasonable risk should be assumed in making overcalls in a suit in which the lead is desired. The importance of obtaining the best lead from partner can hardly be exaggerated in duplicate play, since countless numbers of match points are won and lost in the scoring of extra tricks. If a defender holds a suit headed by A K Q, it is almost obligatory to overcall even though a risk of being set for more than the value of game is thereby incurred. It will be seen that where such a trump suit is held, the likelihood of being doubled is reduced considerably, inasmuch as the highest outstanding trump is the jack.

Where the lead of a suit is not especially desired, caution should be exercised in making overcalls of two in a minor suit, especially when vulnerable. Such overcalls are a frequent target for severe penalty doubles. The making of such a bid many times provides the opponents with "fielder's choice." That is to say, they have the choice of doubling, if that appears more profitable to them; or if you can make the contract, they simply go on with their bidding and your overcall has not served as very much of an obstruction, since it is made at a reasonably low level.

It is to be borne in mind that when you enter the

auction with an overcall, you are apt to induce your partner to enter the fight with a suit of his own. Consequently, one should be very careful in making overcalls on a hand which contains a singleton in some unbid suit which partner may choose to name.

For example:

♠ 10 x x x   ♡ 10   ◇ A Q x x x x   ♣ K x

If the opening bid is 1 heart, a 2 diamond overcall is a reasonable step in duplicate. If partner elects to compete either by raising or by mentioning spades or clubs you should not be in difficulty, but if the opening bid happens to be 1 spade, an overcall of 2 diamonds would be of very doubtful wisdom, since partner may elect to compete in hearts and you have no safety in a return to 3 diamonds. That is another way of saying that one should beware of overcalls when he has length in the suit bid by the opponent.

♠ A K J x   ♡ x x x   ◇ x   ♣ K J 10 x x

The adversaries' opening bid has been 1 heart. The orthodox overcall of 2 clubs is recommended. If partner desires to bid 2 diamonds, you will have a convenient retreat to 2 spades and your distribution will have been shown. In duplicate, competition from partners in part score hands is more to be expected than in rubber bridge. Then there is the further consideration that if the opponents stop at 2 of their suit, you will be able to compete conveniently with a further overcall of 2 spades.

♠ x   ♡ A K J x   ◇ x x x   ♣ K J 10 x x

Over an adverse opening bid of 1 diamond, the recommended overcall is 1 heart. If partner competes with 1 spade, a convenient return bid by you of 2 clubs is available.

Early raises of partner's overcall should be given

more freely in duplicate than in rubber bridge, particularly if a high card is held in his suit. This will permit him safely to lead away from a doubtful holding such as A Q or K J against a final contract.

Furthermore, it will provide him with information which should be helpful to him in determining whether or not to make a sacrifice bid against the opposing contract. This is especially true where your side holds the spade suit. For example:

As South you hold:

♠ K x x x ♡ x x x ◊ Q x x x ♣ x x

The bidding has proceeded as follows:

West	North	East	South
1 ♡	1 ♠	2 ♡	?

A raise to 2 spades is recommended. Such a bid accomplishes the dual purpose of permitting partner to open spades safely should the opponents play the hand and also permits him to take a sacrifice at 4 spades should such action appear judicious to him.

In the earlier chapters of this book it has been pointed out that the partner of the overcaller should never strain to make a bid, inasmuch as overcaller has failed to double, and consequently is not inviting voluntary action from partner. This principle should be relaxed somewhat in duplicate bridge. For example:

As South you hold:

♠ A Q 10 x x ♡ x x ◊ 10 9 x ♣ 9 x x

The bidding has proceeded as follows:

West	North	East	South
1 ◊	2 ♣	Pass	?

In rubber bridge a bid of 2 spades at this point is doubtful strategy, but in duplicate bridge a bid of 2 spades is recommended inasmuch as it is highly unlikely that opener will permit your partner to buy the contract at 2 clubs, and you may feel disposed to compete on a later round when it will be less safe to do so. Furthermore, a bid of 2 spades at this point may inhibit the opener from taking further action which from your standpoint appears to be not especially welcome. The actual hand to which I refer was played in a recent national championship and the complete deal was as follows:

```
                    ♠ ——
                    ♡ Q x x x
                    ◇ A x x
                    ♣ A K J 10 x x
    ♠ J 9 x x   ┌─────────┐   ♠ K x x x
    ♡ A K 2     │    N    │   ♡ J 10 x x
    ◇ K J x x   │  W   E  │   ◇ Q x x
    ♣ Q x       │    S    │   ♣ x x
                └─────────┘
                    ♠ A Q 10 x x
                    ♡ x x
                    ◇ 10 9 x
                    ♣ 9 x x
```

The bidding actually proceeded as follows:

West	North	East	South
1 ◇	2 ♣	Pass	Pass
Double	3 ♣	3 ♡	3 ♠
Pass	4 ♣	Pass	Pass

The contract was defeated 1 trick.

It will be observed that if South had bid 2 spades immediately, West would have been obliged to pass. North would have bid 3 clubs and East would very likely have passed, permitting the fulfillment of contract. If, however, East decided to act, South would be able to pass with perfect ease. He would have done his duty, permitting North to take appropriate action, which in this case would be a profitable penalty double.

I recognize that in the game of bridge generalizations have little value, but for what it may be worth I offer the following: If it is true that at rubber bridge where a doubt exists the pass is usually superior, it is my belief that in duplicate bridge, where a genuine doubt exists, aggressive action will be more profitable. The reason is that there are different goals at stake. In rubber bridge, it is the attainment of total points. In duplicate, it is dogfight for the particular hand. It has been my observation that in match-point duplicate enterprise is rewarded more highly and errors are penalized with less severity. Boards are won not merely by the exercise of sound technique but perhaps more often in profiting by the errors of the opposition. The more you participate in the auction, the greater number of chances do you afford the enemy to commit an error.

Since overcalls are made more freely in duplicate than in rubber bridge it follows, therefore, that rescues of partner's overcalls which have been doubled may be made with greater frequency.

Prompt Action

In match-point duplicate, even more than in rubber bridge, it is fatal to be shut out of the auction with a hand containing moderate values. A situation in which this is apt to occur is where partner's opening bid has been doubled for a takeout by the next opponent. Where you lack sufficient strength for a redouble, it may be vital for you to act at once, especially where participation on a later round may be fraught with danger; or where you may not have time to describe two salient features of your hand.

As South you hold:

♠ x x   ♡ A Q 10 x   ◇ x x x   ♣ Q 10 x x

The bidding has proceeded:

North	East	South
1 ♣	Double	?

What do you do?

I have found it profitable in situations of this type to make an immediate bid of 1 heart. On the next round I am in a position to make a competitive bid in clubs, and partner should realize that my hand is of only moderate strength inasmuch as I had not seen fit to redouble. The bid of 1 heart has the advantage (a) of suggesting what appears to be a good lead should the opponents win the auction; (b) of insuring against being shut out of the heart suit, should partner have four mediocre hearts.

Close Doubles

At rubber bridge you would not dream of making a close double of a contract such as 3 clubs, which if fulfilled will give your opponents game. But in duplicate you may have to risk a doubtful double now and then, as in such bidding as this:

South	West	North	East
1 ♠	Pass	2 ♣	2 ♦
Pass	Pass	2 ♠	Pass
Pass	3 ♦	Pass	Pass
?			

Both sides are vulnerable. You are South and hold:

♠ A Q x x x   ♡ x x x   ♢ K 10 x   ♣ K x

Your side should be able to win five tricks against 3 diamonds, but unexpected breaks might permit East to make the contract. You would never double in rubber bridge and risk having a game made against you, just for the chance of increasing the expected penalty from 100 to 200. But at duplicate you should think of this: You could probably have made the 2 spade contract, which would score 110. If you defeat 3 diamonds one trick undoubled, it will give you only 100 points and you will lose to all the North-South pairs whose opponents did not choose to go to 3 diamonds against them. So you must double to protect your chance to get better than the 110-point score you could have made at 2 spades.

If I were asked what single score produces more swings than any other, when match points are computed, I would unhesitatingly reply: minus 200. While minus 100 many times proves to be a good score (in cases where the adversaries could have made 110, 120, 130, or 140), 200 points exceeds the value of any part score contract and is apt to be disastrous, unless the loss is incurred as a save against a game.

Conversely it follows that plus 200 is one of the best scores attainable and is the figure upon which the duplicate player must frequently fix his aim.

In a dogfight for part score, by two non-vulnerable teams, where you have reached the conclusion that your side can go no farther than 3 hearts and the opposition competes at 3 spades, a double, when only a one-trick set is in view would be unthinkable at rubber bridge, for the extra 50 points thus scored are inadequate compensation for the risk incurred. Even when the opponents are vulnerable and the additional revenue is increased by 100 points, such close doubles should be eschewed when the coin of the realm is the prime objective.

At match-point duplicate entirely different considerations prevail. When the opposition has deprived you of the opportunity to score 140 points, an effort should be exerted to make them pay for their trespass. If they are not vulnerable and you succeed in defeating them only one trick, the compensation of 100 points will be inadequate and your match-point score will probably still be bad. The difference between 50 and 100 points will not be very decisive and such doubles should therefore not be made on suspicion, since a fulfilled doubled contract will surely result in a bottom for you.

Where you are quite confident that you can defeat them one trick, you should double because occasionally you will defeat the contract a trick more than was expected and the 300 points thus attained should land you close to the top.

Where the opponents are vulnerable, regardless of whether or not you are, a somewhat different attitude should be assumed. Since a set of one trick doubled will yield you 200 points, you should be quicker to wield the ax, despite the fact that such practice will occasionally result in a bottom score when the adverse contract is fulfilled. In most such cases it will be found that the "zero" thus incurred was not quite the disaster that it would seem to be at first blush, for in most of these cases you will discover that had the opposition been permitted to play the hand at 3 spades undoubled and scored 140 points, your score would have been well below average, anyhow; so that your loss by doubling was only a few points. Whereas the gain where the double succeeds is much more than just a few points. The percentages, therefore, favor close doubles of vulnerable opponents.

Sacrificing

There is much more sacrifice bidding in duplicate than in rubber bridge. In rubber bridge, a non-vulnerable pair does not deliberately take a 500-point set to keep its opponents from winning the rubber. At best the 500 loss would give it approximately an even break, and perhaps the opponents can be defeated.

In duplicate, a non-vulnerable pair must not overlook an opportunity to stop a vulnerable game by taking a sacrifice of 500, provided it is a fairly sure thing that the opposing game can be made. It doesn't pay, in duplicate, to hope for miracles.

My advice, however, is never to take a doubtful sacrifice. Once you do so you commit yourself to a minus score. If the opponents are permitted to play the hand, there is still the chance that you will be plus. It is my practice never to move deliberately minus while there still remains a chance to be plus. Nor is it my policy to take it for granted that the opponents always make what they have bid.

As a matter of fact, a premature sacrifice bid may prove very effective. For example: the adversary are bidding strongly and appear to be headed for a final contract of 4 hearts. You and partner have participated in spades. If it is your intention to sacrifice at 4 spades, when the adversary arrives there, it might be a good policy to bid 4 spades before they actually reach game. The psychological effect of such procedure is at times surprising. The opposition will sometimes feel from your apparent show of confidence that it is necessary for them to sacrifice at 5 hearts instead of doubling you (don't try this too often).

Sacrifices against slams should be engaged in very sparingly, where the penalty will exceed the value of the adverse game. The reason is that any penalty in excess of the game value will more often than not mean a below-average score for the defender and he will be salvaging very few match points by the "save." These will be made up for by those hands in which the slam is, surprisingly enough, defeated.

The bidding on this deal is fairly typical.

Both sides were vulnerable.

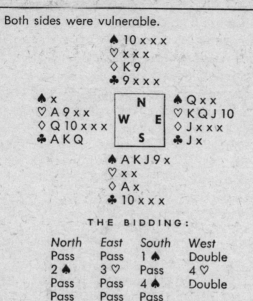

```
                    ♠ 10 x x x
                    ♡ x x x
                    ◇ K 9
                    ♣ 9 x x x
   ♠ x              ┌─────────┐       ♠ Q x x
   ♡ A 9 x x        │    N    │       ♡ K Q J 10
   ◇ Q 10 x x x     │ W     E │       ◇ J x x x
   ♣ A K Q          │    S    │       ♣ J x
                    └─────────┘
                    ♠ A K J 9 x
                    ♡ x x
                    ◇ A x
                    ♣ 10 x x x
```

THE BIDDING:

North	East	South	West
Pass	Pass	1 ♠	Double
2 ♠	3 ♡	Pass	4 ♡
Pass	Pass	4 ♠	Double
Pass	Pass	Pass	

South, vulnerable, would never have bid 4 spades in rubber bridge. The chance of beating 4 hearts is a doubtful one, but enough of a possibility to hope for. South fully realizes that there is no chance of making 4 spades. But at duplicate, knowing that he is most unlikely to go down more than two tricks (500 points) at spades, South considers sacrifice bid a better chance.

The play of this hand, too, was typically in duplicate style. West started off by cashing three club tricks, then East-West took two heart tricks and South was already down two. He had lost the maximum of 500 he had expected. He had to win all the rest of the tricks or he would be down 800 and could not possibly get a good score, whether the opponents could make a vulnerable game or not.

Now South got in by trumping a third round of

hearts. He took the ace of spades. Then he entered dummy with the king of diamonds, led a low spade, and finessed for the queen. By winning the finesse he held the set to 500 points.

There was no "guessing" connected with South's decision to finesse for the queen of spades. If the queen of spades could be dropped by leading the King, North-South could have won two spades and two diamonds against 4 hearts, so the 4 heart contract could not have been made. In that case, even the score of down 500 would be a bad one. South had to assume that 4 hearts could have been made, in which case West had to have a singleton spade and the finesse would work.

Fourth-Hand Openings

Certain holdings which might be "tossed in" at rubber bridge by the player in the fourth seat are justifiable openings in duplicate. However, the range of difference is very narrow, and liberties should be taken, as a rule, only with hands that have some values in the spade suit, to guard against painful competition from the adversaries in that direction.

My observation has been that sub-minimum openings, fourth hand, are a losing practice. While an occasional good score will be obtained by such ventures, I am convinced that on balance the net result will be below average. When such openings are made, you are more apt to run into adverse competition, and you will be at a psychological disadvantage in exercising your judgment in making future decisions. Any further action on your part will be colored with the apprehension induced by your doubtful opening.

In most duplicates you will be handed a convention card in which are to be inscribed outlines of artificial

bids employed by the participants. My suggestion is
that you ask your opponents for a clarification before
the start of play. And if you keep your own conventions
to a minimum you will minimize your own chores when
the adversaries make their inquiries.

APPENDIX II

The New Scale of
IMP (*International Match Points*) *Score*

IMPS	OLD SCALE	NEW SCALE
1	20–60	20–40
2	70–130	50–80
3	140–210	90–120
4	220–340	130–160
5	350–490	170–210
6	500–740	220–260
7	750–990	270–310
8	1000–1240	320–360
9	1250–1490	370–420
10	1500–1990	430–490
11	2000–2490	500–590
12	2500–2990	600–690
13	3000–3490	700–790
14	3550–3990	800–890
15	4000–and more	900–1040
16		1050–1190
17		1200–1340
18		1350–1490
19		1500–1740
20		1750–1990
		2000 points and over; 1 IMP for every 250 points difference.

Contract Bridge Scoring Table

TRICK POINTS FOR CONTRACTORS

	Undoubled	Doubled
Clubs or Diamonds each	20	40
Hearts or Spades, each	30	60
No Trump { first	40	80
No Trump { each subsequent	30	60

Redoubling doubles the trick points. 100 trick points constitute a game.

UNDERTRICK PENALTIES

	Not Vulnerable	Vulnerable
Undoubled, each	50	100
Doubled { first	100	200
Doubled { each subsequent	200	300

PREMIUMS

	Not Vulnerable	Vulnerable
Overtricks		
Undoubled, each	trick value	trick value
Doubled, each	100	200
Redoubled, each	200	400
Making a doubled or		
redoubled contract	50	50
Slams bid and won		
Little	500	750
Grand	1000	1500

Honors in one hand

4 Trump honors	100
5 Trump honors or	
4 Aces at No Trump	150

Rubber Bonus

Two game	700
Three game	500

Unfinished Rubber—winners of one game score 300 points. If but one side has a part score in an unfinished game, it scores 50 points. Doubling and redoubling do not affect Honor, Slam, or Rubber points. Vulnerability does not affect points for Honors.

CHARLES H. GOREN

NEW REVISED

POINT COUNT BIDDING

AT A GLANCE

POINT COUNT TABLE

Ace—4 points   King—3 points   Queen—2 points

Jack—1 point

    Add one point for all four Aces

    Deduct one point for Aceless hand

Quick Tricks: A K (2)   A Q (1½)   K Q (1)   K x (½)

POINT COUNT TABLE FOR DISTRIBUTION

For Opening Bids:	When Raising partner's bid:
count	count
3 points for void	5 points for void
2 points for singleton	3 points for singleton
1 point for doubleton	1 point for doubleton
	(provided you have adequate trump support)

When raising your partner, deduct one point with only three trumps.

Deduct one point if distribution is 4–3–3–3.

To determine the value of a hand, add high card points to distribution points.

26 points are normally required to produce **game in a major suit; 28–29 points** in a **minor.**

33 points will generally produce a **small slam.**

37 points will almost invariably produce a **grand slam.**

REQUIREMENTS FOR OPENING BIDS

One in a Suit

14 point hands must be opened.

13 point hands may be opened, if a good rebid is available.

All openings must contain 2 quick tricks.

A third position opening is permitted with 11 points if hand contains a good suit.

When you have more than one biddable suit, length determines the choice. If the suits are of unequal length, bid the longer one first. If you have two five-card suits, you should bid first the higher ranking, not necessarily the stronger.

Biddable Suit

The weakest four-card major suit which opener is permitted to bid is one headed by at least the King and Jack. In other words, your four-card trump suit must contain at least four high card points in the suit itself.

A five-card suit is biddable even though it contains no high-card strength in the suit.

Two in a Suit—(Demand)

25 points with good 5-card suit

23 points with good 6-card suit

21 points with good 7-card suit

(1 point less with 2nd good 5-card suit)

With **19 to 21** points—open One of a suit. Over partner's response, jump in NT.

No Trump (Count High Card values only)

1 NT—**16** to **18** points

2 NT—**22** to **24** points

3 NT—**25** to **27** points

OPENING BIDS OF 3 AND 4

These are called pre-emptive bids and designate weak hands. A pre-emptive bid must never contain more than ten high card points. **Partner** of pre-emptive bidder should not raise partner unless he can produce 3 or 4 tricks for him.

RESPONSES TO OPENING BIDS

Responses to bid of 1 in a suit, with balanced hand, bid

1 NT with **6** to **10** points
2 NT with **13** to **15** points
3 NT with **16** to **18** points

With Unbalanced Hand

Raise partner's suit bid: To 2 with 7 to 10 points and trump support (trump support consists of Q x x, x x x x).
To 3 with 13 to 16 points and 4 trumps.
To 4 with no more than 9 points in high cards and 5 trumps.
Make a jump shift with 19 points.

Show a New Suit:

At 1 level with 6 points or more
At 2 level with 10 points or more

Responses to bid of 2 in a suit:
With 6 points or less, bid 2 NT
With 7 points or more make a positive response

SUIT RESPONSE TO 1 NT

With Unbalanced Hand

The Two Club Convention: A response of 2 clubs shows 8 points, or more, at least one 4-card major suit—and asks partner to show his major suit.
A response of 2 D, or 2 H or 2 S shows less than 8 points and a 5-card suit.
With 10 points and a good suit, jump to 3 of that suit.
Bid 4 of a major with a very long suit, but less than 10 high card points.

Suit Response to 2 NT

Bid 3 clubs with 4 points or more, plus a 4-card major suit.

Bid a 5-card major suit headed by an honor, plus 4 points. Show any 6-card suit.

Suit Response to 3 NT

Bid any suit of 5 cards or more, if hand contains 5 points in high cards.

No Trump Response
to 1 NT Opening
Bid 2 NT with 8–9 points.
    (7 points with 5-card suit)
  3 NT with 10–14 points.
  4 NT with 15–16 points.
  6 NT with 17–18 points.
  7 NT with 21 points.

No Trump Response
to 2 NT Opening
Bid 3 NT with 4–8 points.
  4 NT with 9–10 points.
  6 NT with 11–12 points.

No Trump Response
to 3 NT Opening
Bid 4 NT with 7 points.
  6 NT with 8–9 points.
  7 NT with 12 points.

REBIDS BY OPENING BIDDER

After Partner Has Made His Original Response

If you have 13–16 Points—Minimum Hand

  Pass 1 NT response (unless hand is unbalanced)

  Rebid your own suit

  Rebid in a new suit at 1-level does not require additional values.

  Rebid in a new suit at 2-level if it can be done cheaply.

  Single raise of partner's suit may be made if your hand is valued at 14–16 points in support of partner.

If you have 16–19 Points—Good Hand

  Make a jump rebid in your own suit if it is a good 6-card suit.

  Offer partner a jump raise in his suit with 4 trumps.

Rebid 2 NT when partner has responded with 2 of a suit with 15–18 points and 3 NT with 19–20 points.

Raise partner's 2-over-1 response to the 3-level.

If you have 19–21 Points—Very Good Hand

Jump to game in partner's major suit response (with 4 trumps)

Jump to game in your own major (6- or 7-card suit)

19–20 points—jump to 2 NT over partner's 1-over-1 response.

21 points—jump to 3 NT over partner's 1-over-1 response.

22 points and up—jump shift in new suit, forcing to game and suggesting slam.

REBIDS BY OPENING NO TRUMP BIDDER

When responder bids 2 clubs, the (2-Club Convention), the opening bidder must show a 4-card biddable major suit if he has one.

With 4 spades	he bids 2 spades.
With 4 hearts	he bids 2 hearts.
With both majors	he bids 2 spades.
With no major	he bids 2 diamonds.

Opening No Trump Bidder Must Pass:

when responder raises to 2 NT and opener has a minimum of 16 points.

when responder bids 2 diamonds, 2 hearts or 2 spades and opener has only 16–17 points and no good fit for responder's suit.

when responder bids 3 NT, 4 spades or 4 hearts.

REBIDS BY RESPONDER

6 to 10 points—Minimum Hand

With 6 points, do not act again, unless partner forces.

With 8–10 points, you should act again if partner offers some inducement.

10 to 13 points—Good Hand

These hands normally are worth 2 bids.

16 to 18 points—Powerful Hand

Bid 3 NT with a balanced hand, or bid a new suit and then jump the bid on the next round. These bids show more than an opening bid.

19 points and up—Slam Zone

Make a Jump Shift at once by bidding one more than necessary in a new suit.

OVERCALLS

The important consideration is the possession of a good suit. This is more important than the number of points held. An overcall should rarely be made in a suit you do not want your partner to lead.

The overcall of 1 NT shows 16–18 points, including a sound stopper in opponent's suit.

The overcall of 2 NT shows the strength of an opening bid of 2 NT.

A jump overcall is preemptive, showing a maximum of 9 high card points based on a hand that will produce within 3 tricks of the bid not vulnerable, or 2 tricks vulnerable.

RESPONSES BY PARTNER OF OVERCALLER

Raise only when you think there is a chance for game.

In supporting partner's overcall, you may do so with less

than normal trump support, for the overcall designates a
very sound suit.

Remember, in responding to partner's overcall, a new suit
by you is not forcing. Nor is a jump raise forcing. It may
frequently be necessary for you to go directly to game if
you think you can make it.

Don't try to rescue your partner's overcall simply because
you cannot support his suit.

TAKEOUT-DOUBLE

When you contemplate a takeout double, you should be
confident that your hand is about as good as the opening
bidder's—at least 13 points.

To double an opening bid of 1 NT, you should have at least
16 points.

Valuing your hand when partner has made a takeout double:

6 points—Fair hand

9 points—Good hand

11 points—probable game.

When Partner's Opening Bid Has Been Doubled

With a good hand—redouble.

Weak hand—pass

With a moderate hand—make the natural bid immediately.

Remember These Values:

Ace—4 points   King—3 points   Queen—2 points
Jack—1 point

Add one point for all four Aces

Deduct one point for Aceless hand

Quick Tricks: A K (2)   A Q (1½)   K Q (1)   K x (½)